W9-CPC-767

TRAN

The Vikings

The Vikings

Text by **O. Madsen**

Translated by David Macrae

Minerva

Table of contents.

Crédits - ATA 8, 12, 13, 15, 28, 29a, b, 32 a, 40, 42, 43, 47, 57, 74, 94, 114 - Baudin/Viollet 120 - Cabaud/Fotogram 4, 9, 10, 11, 72 - Fiore 30b, 33, 34 b, 35, 36, 53, 68, 109, 126, 128 - Fotogram 17 - Germain 20, 23, 38, 80, 83, 84 - Giraudon 65, 86, 124, 144 - Hurault 89 - Lundh/Viollet 48 - ND end papers, 38, 135, 137a, b - Ollivier 117, 131 - Osterreichische Nationalbibliothek Vienne 122 - P2/Ricciarini 54, 58, 127 - SEF 14, 24, 25b, 26, 27, 46, 60, 91, 125, 142a - Simion 132 - Unedi 32b, 44, 45, 63, 69, 71, 73, 106 - Viollet 18, 19a, 22, 25a, 34a, 51, 92, 95, 97, 98, 99, 101, 103, 105, 110, 113, 115, 141c, 142b - Weber/Fotogram 7.

© Editions Minerva, S.A., Genève, 1976
Printer, Industria Gráfica, S.A.
Tuset, 19   Barcelona
San Vicente dels Horts 1976
Depósito legal B. 30359-1976
Printed in Spain

1/ Life among the Vikings

Viking means *king of the sea,* from the work *vik* (bay, gulf) and *kong, kiney* or *king,* meaning the most powerful man' (from the root *ken,* knowledge, power). In Old Norse, the corresponding term was *Vikingr.*

For a long time the Vikings were called by names which meant *men from the North,* such as *Norman.* Or rather this was the name used to describe them by the peoples living to the south, who were amazed and mystified at the appearance of these wild strangers from Denmark, Sweden and Norway.

These warriors seemed to be of the same race and adored the same gods. The earliest northern gods were called *Baal* (Sun), *Balder* (goodness), *Thor* (strength, thunder). According to Are Frode, the first Icelandic historian, Odin, who should be regarded as the king of the gods, as the principle of all things (Alfader), did not reach the north until 65-66 BC, while seeking to escape from the Romans.

In contrast to Greek and Roman mythology which, though of restricted scope, was made famous by the poets, the mythology of Odin, with its somber, bloodthirsty gods, remained unknown for a very long time in the West. Apparently these gods were better suited to the north. The victorious Vikings never thought of transplanting them in the south. When they settled elsewhere they quickly adopted the mode of worship and customs of their new

Inscriptions on a runic stone. Right: figurehead of a Viking vessel.

5

23.233

A Norwegian fjord.

country.

Since peoples have a habit of arranging their own religion, they make sure it is in harmony with their ideas and their tastes; later on, religion becomes more firmly established, takes root and eventually reacts, in turn, on the national character.

Odinism was based on the principle that strength takes precedence in all matters, including both human and divine law.

The Scyths and Germanic tribes, like the Scandinavians, believed that their divinities, which were essentially warlike, liked to intervene in battle. According to Tacitus, one of them once said: "Bravery is the only true human value. God is on the side of the strongest".

Viking warriors, with their amazing physical vigor and skill in the martial arts, felt that there was nothing higher than their courage and, when speaking of their enemies, would say: "Even if they were stronger than the gods, I would still fight them."

Saxon the Grammarian quotes the following words of defiance addressed by a proud Scandinavian to Odin, with whom he was comparing himself: "So where is he, the famous Odin, the fearsome hero who has but one eye to guide him. Ah! if only I could see this dreaded spouse of Frigga! His splendid shield and mighty war-horse will be of little use to him; he will not go unscathed if he emerges from his abode in Lethro. It is permitted to attack and to fight a warrior-god."

When the faith of the early years began to wane, the people still continued to worship the principle of force. The ancient story of Olaüs, king of Norway, tells us how a warrior who was being urged to convert to Christianity replied: "You must know that I believe in neither idols nor spirits. I have travelled in a number of countries and have met giants and monstrous men, all of whom have failed to defeat me. Therefore, to this day, I believe only in my strength and my courage."

The gods were respected by the people only because they were endowed with superhuman strength and because they had a weapon which was without equal—thunder. Their religion aroused warlike feelings of vengeance and utter disregard for human life.

The greatest happiness of the gods and the inhabitants of Valhalla was to hack each other to bits in savage combat all day long. In real life, where armed struggle was the most normal state of affairs, the development of the body was the main component of education. From the earliest age, the young were taught to leap huge distances, climb over jagged and dangerous rocks, build up their resistance and generally become accustomed to the state of war. As soon as adolescents were strong enough to wield a weapon, they became emancipated: having hitherto been a member solely of their own family, they now belonged to

7

the State.

The supremacy of strengh over all other qualities was even recognized by law. Weak men were not entitled to own property since they would not be able to defend it. Victory was a sure sign that the gods were on one's side.

A man's worth was measured by his strength and courage. One of the Danish kings promised promotion to high rank in his army to any man who attacked the enemy immediately when faced by only one adversary, who stood his ground when attacked by two, who retreated only one step when attacked by three and who fled only when four men descended on him at the same time.

Besides being a disgrace, cowardice was also a crime. According to one of the sagas, Harald the Blue, in a town which he had founded, made it an offense to utter the word *fear,* even in the midst of great danger.

A man who had fled and thrown away his shield or who had been wounded from behind did not dare to show his face again. Capture by the enemy, even after a brave defense, was a dishonor. Forthon, king of Denmark, was taken prisoner at the height of a battle. When his captors offered to spare his life, he refused, saying: "What good is life if it be spent in shame? Even if you were to return my treasures and my crown, how could you restore my honor, since it is now lost? Your generosity could

8

not bring back my glory and future generations will say: "Forthon was taken alive by the enemy!"

The word for coward, *niting,* was an instant cause for a duel to the death, as the injuries done by words were felt to be the most serious.

The Icelanders had made up a number of songs which were distinctly unflattering to Harald, who promptly sent a fleet to punish them. It is thought that the law whereby any Icelander who composed satires about the kings of the three Scandinavian States was punishable by death dates from about this time.

There was a virtually uninterrupted sequence of fighting between individual men, tribes and peoples; a warrior whose life was not taken in battle often committed suicide in order to to win, in Valhalla, the glory due to those who die violently.

If a father was in danger of death from old age or sickness, it was thought that bludgeoning him to death was an act of piety, as Odin never forgave the shame of a natural death. A man had to die by force of arms, and greet death with a smile on his lips.

An officer of one of the Norwegian kings praised his master by saying: "Henceforth, the world will say that my master died laughing!

Ilacquin, king of Norway, condemned to death seven warriors from an army which had been sent against him. Before behead-

Landscape in southern Norway. Right: Viking burial-place in Sweden.

ing them, Thorschill asked them what they thought about death, now that they were confronted with it. The first of them replied: "Why should I be afraid of what has already happened to my father and what was, in any case, going to happen to me also, sooner or later?" The second replied: "Fear is forbidden by law. I shall never be heard uttering a word of fear." The third, staring Thorschill straight in the eye, replied: "I am glad to die; I would sooner die a glorious death like mine than live a shameful life like yours." The fourth made this highly unusual reply: "I accept death with courage and pleasure. All I ask is that my head be cut off as soon as possible. Men have often wondered whether, after decapitation, a man's body still has any feeling. Let's see: I shall take this knife in my hand; if, after my head has been cut off, I raise it against you, that will be proof that I have not lost all feeling; but if I drop it, it will prove the opposite; so

strike quickly in order to resolve the matter once and for all." The fifth replied: "Facing death, I mock my enemies." The sixth said: "Strike me in the face; I defy you to make me show the slightest sign of fear, or even to make me flinch." The seventh replied: "I welcome death, since I have witnessed the deaths of all my comrades and it would be cruel for me to survive them."

However, besides feelings of vigorous hatred and implacable vengeance, the hearts of these semi-barbarous warriors were also capable of the most cordial friendship and loyal devotion.

The shared experience of danger and adventure forged bonds of brotherhood among them and produced a strong sense of loyalty, to the point where a man would give his own life to save that of a friend. What was known as the *pact of brothers,* commonly found in the North, meant that, when setting off on an expedition, men

10

Left: the god of fertility. Above: amulet.

would bind themselves to a given chief by swearing not to live on if he should die.

Warriors sometimes formed an association among themselves whereby they agreed to protect, defend and avenge each other, and even to risk their lives in each other's service.

Fraternity in arms was certainly known in the ancient world; in Greece, examples of it have been reported from Homer's time. Chivalry, which was the same fraternity in arms, only on a vaster scale, was simply an advanced form of these associations, which are mentioned so frequently by chroniclers and poets. However, the *fraternity in arms* flourished most particularly in the North, where evidence of it has been found from the remote past. Far from abolishing such associations, Christianity gave them a special hallowed status, as *confraternities*.

After friendship, perhaps we should say a word or two about love, which must surely occur in all countries and throughout all periods of history in one form or another.

In the North, love may be slower to manifest itself, but when it does appear, it lasts longer. It may also have given rise to fewer excesses and more acts of heroism.

Odin was something like the Mercury of Antiquity, who was regarded as the god of thieves. For him, wealth was always meritorious, no matter how it was acquired; for a rich man, the doors of Valhalla were always wide open. Whereas Christ, in the Sermon on the Mount, said: "Blessed are the poor!", Odin would have been more inclined to say: "Blessed are the rich!"

The Vikings had brought so much treasure from their plunderous raids and victorious battles, to a country where it was not really possible to spend such wealth, that, when Christianity preached charity in the newly converted North, those pious persons who wished to give alms found that there were no poor people in Scandinavia to give them to; they therefore had to look for them abroad!

Size was mainly what gave Scandinavian dwellings their status in society; the palace of Ingolph, according to Arngrimus, was for example, 105 feet long.

Fighting, eating and drinking were what one needed in order to be happy, both in Valhalla and on earth.

On special occasions, the floor was usually covered with straw. Smoke from the fire-place, which was situated in the middle of the room, was evacuated through a hole in the roof or the wall. Benches were placed along the table, which was often very long. The king and queen occupied the place of honor *(högsäte)* in the middle of the bench, facing the sun. The most distinguished guest sat opposite them. The men and women

14

sat in pairs and drank together. Toasts
were drunk from one end of the table
another and the beer had to be passed
across the fire. According to the sagas,
the goblets used to be emptied in a single
gulp. Those that have been found are so
huge that modern man would be incapable
of drinking that much beer and is thus
clearly the inferior of his ancient forbears,
in physical terms. Great banquets were held
mainly before the Vikings set out on an
expedition, in order to plan the operation,

and afterwards, to celebrate its success.

Agriculture was not neglected in this
early period, though it was not held in very
high esteem.

Samples of early Viking art-work, including carved and engraved stone, have
been found. During the long winter nights,
the Vikings soon began to carve objects
out of wood. Silver birch, in particular, was
used to make some perfectly charming
objects. Among the objects which have been
recovered are a number of remarkably

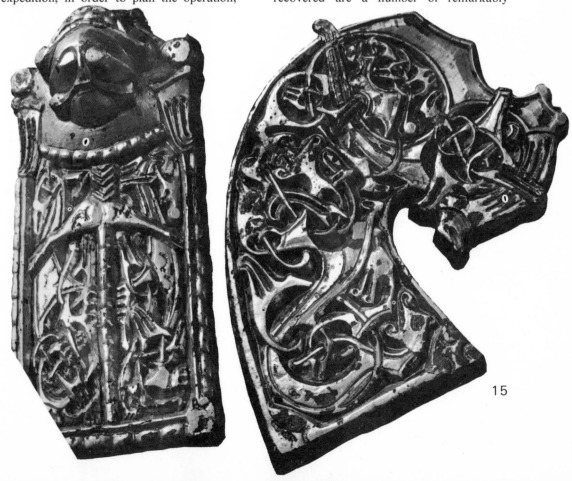

finely carved pieces of ornamental panelling, some of which depict heroes in battle.

For this nation of seafarers, a study of the stars was clearly very important. In one of the sagas, a young man describes all his talents to his beautiful fiancée: he could wrestle, skate, swim, sing, and he knew the names of each of the stars. These names were quite unrelated to the ones we use today. The Great Bear was the *Big Dog;* Orion was *Frigga's Distaff,* while the Milky Way was the *Wintry Way.*

The year began at the winter solstice, and was divided into quarters and months, the months being further divided into weeks of seven days; the days were divided into 12 parts, each with a special name.

The longest night of winter was thought of as the *Mother Night,* since the Vikings believed that the world had been created during that night and that all the other nights come from it. Indeed, time was counted in nights, not days. This ancient custom also occurred in certain Germanic tribes, and is thought to have survived in the form of certain common expressions which are in use in the Scandinavian countries today.

Historians have tried to dispel some of the clouds surrounding the history of the Vikings first political institutions. It is interesting to note that, while despotism seemed to be the prime form of political organization among the ancient peoples of Asia, freedom flourished in the north.

Norwegian fjord.

16

Clearly, the lure of the courtly life was lost on a people which lived through hunting and fishing. What these warlike folk most needed was a clever, fearless chief who would lead them to victory. The man chosen for the job was the bravest. There are three places in Denmark where, according to tradition, the king was elected. At each of them, a dozen pieces of rock are arranged in a circle. In the middle, there is a higher piece of rock carved like a throne.

The choice was usually made from among the members of the royal family. The early Viking kings claimed to be descended from the gods. The chiefs proclaimed the name which had won their support, while the common people showed their reaction either by howling with dismay, or by striking their shields rhythmically as a sign of approval.

Left and above: the Viking burial-place at Lindhom Høje, in Jutland (Denmark). Below: a Danish warrior (motif on cauldron of repoussé metal).

2/ The everyday life and the institutions of the Vikings

Because of the harsh northern climate, the large areas of rugged mountainous terrain, and the barrenness of certain other regions, the land in which the Vikings lived was rather poor. The proximity of the seas, the fjords and immense lakes had given these hardy northeners a taste for adventure at sea.

Quite early in their history, they sought in sea-borne conquest the wealth which Nature had denied them on land. In Scandinavia, boats have been discovered which were from the prehistoric period. Once the Vikings had become skilled navigators and, particularly, when their numbers had grown, they ventured far away from their native shores in their quest for wealth. One successful expedition lead to another. Once they had grown accustomed to the maritime life, they had no reason to fear bad weather, which in any case had more than once left them stranded on foreign shores from which they had returned richly laden with booty. The frightened inhabitants bought them off with precious metals when they were unable to drive them off by force of arms.

Whenever they appeared, the Vikings were regarded as monsters from hell, whose sole companions were the demons of murder and fire. More often than not, the fear they instilled in the local people very nearly sufficed, on its own, to bring the Vikings victory. Seeking protection and divine intercession against this scourge, the priests added a verse to the litanies:

"*A furore Normannorum libera nos, Domine* (From the fury of the North-men deliver us oh Lord!)"

Plunder on this scale had never been seen before—certainly not in so many countries. The chronicles of the monasteries paint a vivid picture of the devastation and terror they spread wherever they went.

Historians have often discussed the causes of the emigration of so many thousands of Scandinavians, who left their countries at the same time and went off in all directions, in unrelated bands, seeking adventures in remote places, despite the perils of the sea, and leaving behind them a trall of desolation.

One thing, however, is certain, as the early historians themselves recognized: in the words of Guillaume de Jumièges: "the Danes became so numerous that, eventually, each of their islands were full of men; many of them were forced to emigrate by virtue of laws enacted by their kings; another reason for their growth was the fact the men readily mated with many women. When their sons grew up, their father sent them all away, except one, whom he made his heir".

The North was full of powerful lords, or petty kings, with a variety of titles. *Herse* was a title even higher than that of *Jarl* or count. Obviously the herse would have been reluctant to see his states diminish by having them shared out among so many sons; so he would choose the strongest, the one most capable of upholding the honor

Early tapestry.

Hood from Viking garment (10th century) found in Greenland.

of the race, sometimes by drawing lots; the rest of his sons would then be dismissed, and given ships, men and weapons with which to seek their fortune elsewhere.

War was a permanent state. The vanquished, and those sent into exile, enrolled in the Viking bands. When Harold with the Fair Hair had assembled under his rule all the minor states of Norway, the dispossessed lords were dispatched to try their luck in some other country.

At this point, the defeated princes, the luckless sons of herses who had not been chosen as their father's heir, those who had been banished for various reasons and adventure-seekers of all sorts, used to assemble and unite their forces to form fleets which, because of their size, were all the more awesome; under the command of a man specially chosen for his courage, they would then set off in search of booty or conquest.

The wandering warrior, or *wargr,* became a sea-king, *Soekong* or *Viking*; when several of them joined forces, they chose a king of kings, or *Kongakong.*

A Scandinavian funeral urn in the shape of a house.

The Vikings chose stormy nights on which to set sail, and showed a complete mastery of seamanship as they rode over the waves towards distant lands, where they either went ashore at random or chose the most fertile regions.

Once these intrepid sailors had taken their craft into the mouth of some river, often overcoming great navigational obstacles in so doing, they left it in a sheltered cove or inlet until it was needed again.

On land, they took to horseback, having first raided the stables of castles, monas-teries or farms. Brigades of armed men, in this improvised fashion, routed both serfs, who fought on foot, and knights who were on horseback; in all cases, the element of surprise played a large part in the Viking victory.

The visitor to Copenhagen can see the remarkable weapons the Vikings used, such as their enormous, massive swords, the handle of which was decorated with inter-woven shapes and silver dragons.

Since Christianity had denounced the Viking gods, they took their revenge by

23

Below: Ancient Swedish urn. Right: Viking tomb at Kivik (Sweden).

24

Facing: painted stones, Kivik.

massacring priests and monks. They did not confine themselves to night raids, but went openly after the big cities, taking London, and laying siege to Paris. They even had plans for the conquest of Rome and Constantinople.

Though the literature of the countries which they visited often painted a grim picture of the Vikings, the poetry of the Nordic countries has used the most brilliant colors to depict these peerless warriors, these kings of the sea, who went off to conquer whole kingdoms and seize huge piles of loot, from which they then offered crowns, jewels to the woman they adorned.

Listen, for a moment, to the plaintive song of the fiancée, as she sadly and anxiously awaits her lover's return: "Oh! winds of heaven, greet my beloved with your loud voice; oh hail, take my message to him; clouds tell him how much I miss him; oh sky, give him intelligence and wisdom; oh vapors of the air, tell him of my love and the longing in my heart!"

Left: stele of engraved stone, Haggeby (Uppland). Above and below: motifs from stone found in Gotland.

In a poem by Tegner, whose work is so famous in the Nordic world, Frithiof says:

"Free sea! you know no master who can keep you subdued at his will. Your king is the warrior who never flinches, however high you raise your angry foaming waves; the hero delights in your vast azure plains. His ship cuts across them like the blade of a plow, and the rain of blood which falls in the shadow of the masts becomes for it a seed as brilliant as steel. It can be seen rising like a harvest of glory and gold. Be faithful to me, wild waves, I shall follow you. The burial mound of my father lies in a peaceful spot, and the waves murmur around its green grass. But my tomb will be blue, crowned by the foam of the sea; it will float for ever among the mists and the storms, luring others to sink into the abyss with it. You who have been my dwelling during my life-time, you will be my tomb when I am dead, oh free sea!"

Historians from both Norway and Sweden have praised the Vikings, contribution to the progress of civilization.

It has even been claimed that the origins and characteristics of medieval chivalry lie in the piracy practised by the North-men. Even when one makes ample allowance for differences of place, surroundings and local customs, it remains true that the Vikings used to slaughter priests and women in the churches, reduce the unarmed peasants to slavery, and generally burn, loot and steal everything wherever they went, whether

28

they did it by force, cunning or surprise. Surely this is the exact opposite of the feelings of chivalry the medieval knights were supposed to have had.

Far from being a matter for discussion by the mere assertion of opposing arguments, this is one which can be checked against the facts, which show that the Vikings were often cruel and treacherous. The most one cay say in this respect is that they were both brigands and heroes.

Some of them were men of great merit and genius, who, having horrified the world with

their cruel acts, then turned away from war, and became great and just princes, even saints. It is important to distinguish between the time when they followed the principles of Odin, and the later period following their energetic espousal of the precepts of Christianity.

Nordic authors sometimes claim that the Vikings had perfected the arts of war to a level unknown in the rest of Europe. They have laid great stress on the society of Jomsvikings, at Jomsborg, in Pomerania. Membership in this society was restricted to males between the ages of 15 and 50. Any man who, in an evenly balanced combat, had backed down was ineligible for membership or was expelled. The town of Jomsborg was inhabited solely by Vikings; no women or children were allowed in, and no man could leave for more than three days. All the members of this society regarded each other as brothers-in-arms, and were obliged to defend each other. No-one was allowed to take the law into his own hands; the chief's decision was binding on all. All loot was given to him and he alone was entitled to share it out. Each member had to report what he had learnt to the chief. Accurate information about the countries to be invaded was most important and the giving of false information was a severely punished crime.

Of course, no-one doubts that the society of Jomsvikings was a great military school, but, out of the countless Vikings who flooded

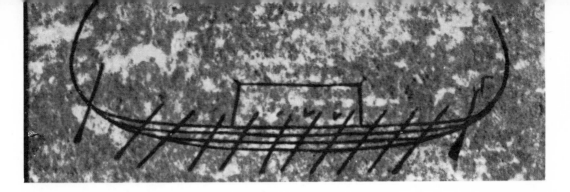

into Europe, how many can have come from the Pomeranian school?

The Vikings plainly felt a strong need to organize themselves and to have a chief to lead them on their great expeditions. But it hardly seems fair to claim that the Nordic countries were the only place in Europe where there was an important military school.

Danish authors, who praise the Northmen's ability to organize vast armies, are wrong to attribute to them the institutional structure adopted by the kings of Sweden, Norway and Denmark in their kingdoms, where the king, at the head of the hierarchy, apportioned various roles to the nobility and other castes.

Left: Ornamental motif from Danish stele and vase. Above: one of the earliest pictures of a Viking vessel. (Gotland, 5th century). Below: cist from tomb.

Left: glass pieces from a game, and handle of an 8th-century bronze sword. Above: Viking house at Trelleborg (Denmark).

Reconstitution of a fortified Viking camp at Trelleborg and view of same. Right: the west gate of the camp.

3/ Women in the North

The status of women in Viking society is particularly interesting.

In the vast northern solitude, surrounded by huge lakes, human settlements were thinly spread out, as they are today. The family felt a need to live close together in those days; they lived in a *gâard,* a single house made up of separate apartments, with large secondary buildings.

With his greater strength, the man dominated the household, and was responsible for the protection of those who, for reasons of age or sex, could not protect themselves. The father acted like a king within his own household. Union and strength provided the power of the household. On his father's death, the eldest son inherited the head of the family's fortune and the authority that went with it. Women remained in a state of perpetual minority.

Curiously, however, even though they were pronounced unfit for the lowliest public office, women were still recognized as being capable of reigning over the entire kingdom.

During the early stages of the societies of both north and south Europe, the king seems to have shared to some extent in the divine power. The Pythonissa, the Sybil and the Vestal figured prominently in the religion of both Greeks and Romans. In the grim and bloody mythology of the Nordic countries, the goddesses enjoyed a place next to the gods. The *Vala,* or priestess of Odin, lived in his temple; she was thought to be in touch with the world of the supernatural and to have the gift of prophecy. She was a very powerful woman, who was consulted on all important matters; her voice was regarded as an oracle.

This sacred virgin, or female *skalde,* followed the warriors into battle, stimulated their courage with her song, celebrated victory, and entoned the *drapa,* or funeral song of a glorious death, as appropriate.

Since she was venerated as a supernatural being, she was denied physical love on earth. Woe betide anyone who had loved her or who had been loved by her!— the indignant people would have cut such a sacrilegious and impious man to ribbons.

Once Christianity had stripped the Vala of her dual prestige as a sacred priestess and prophetess, her function declined to that of a magician. Belief in witchcraft and magic was strong among the Vikings.

Nordic women have a very special kind of beauty, with their golden hair, blue eyes, and the brilliant whiteness and purity of their complexion. It has been observed that, out of the various types of beauty found among the European peoples, Scandinavian beauty is closest of all to the classic Greek sculpture, with its cleanness of profile, preciseness of feature and general perfection of design.

Women who betrayed their husbands were cruelly punished; often, a women in such a position would stab to death the adulterous male who had deceived her.

Remains of the foundations of a building at Trelleborg.

37

Viking women were very hard-working; during the long winter evenings they would work away—whether in a king's palace or a poor man's, sewing and embroidering. Brynhild depicted the famous exploits of Sigurd in gold thread, and the daughters of Regner Lodbrog embroidered a picture of a crow on a famous flag which later became the object of an idolatrous cult. A piece of ordinary handwoven fabric was a gift which even a queen would accept with pleasure.

Scandinavian marriage was not solemnized in public ceremonies. Having first obtained the consent of the young woman, the suitor then proceeded either to buy her or abduct her during the night.

It was more honorable for a woman to be bought than abducted. The price paid to the head of the family was the *mundr;* these ancient customs from the sagas have survived in the *hendradagsgal,* or 'gift of the following day', and the *heragaf,* or 'gift offered to the bride'. This Germanic custom

Jewel and silver bracelets (Gotland, 9th century).

Woman's head on Viking jewel.

spread to other countries in the West, so that when Clovis, king of France, asked for the hand of Clotilde, he sent messengers to offer her, as the price of her beauty, and her virtue, a symbolic coin.

Marriage by abduction was more popular among the young warriors, who were proud to conquer girls who were renowned for both their beauty and their lineage.

The castles in which the lords lived were genuine fortresses, built on almost inaccessible high ground. The tall and thick walls which surrounded them were known by a name which could loosely be translated as 'dragon'. Before setting out on an expedition, the master of the house would put his wife and daughters in a safe place. Writers of the modern period, unaware of the meanings which the ancient words once had, have written lurid tales of gentle damsels guarded by dragons and horrible snakes, who were eventually delivered from captivity by the valor of the dashing young warriors who overcame the monsters in question.

The Vikings, who were constantly on the move and often far from home, could not understand marriage in the same way as the burghers or peasants who lived, from one generation to another, in the gâards.

Everything was to be won by the sword— and women ranked high among the booty the warriors brought from their raids and barbarous invasions. Lasting conjugal union, however, was probably less what they had in mind than a mere passing association.

Rather than stoop to making an actual request for the hand of a beautiful and renowned princess, thus risking the father's refusal, a proud young warrior would go to war, fighting his rivals, killing the father

if necessary, and seizing the girl as one treasure among many. According to the *Kianisingasaga,* a Swedish pirate named Gunna went to attack king Reynald in Norway. Before confronting his enemy, the king decided to put his daughter in a safe underground chamber, with food, water and his treasure. Then, in order to conceal her whereabouts even better, he had the soil above her plowed over.

Reynald died in the ensuing battle, the victor discovered the hiding place, married the princess and took the treasure as a dowry.

A warrior who was unequalled in combat could not tolerate rivalry in love. The most beautiful women seemed to belong, by right, to the bravest men.

The young women listened, enthralled, to accounts of bravery and adventure, and fell in love with the heroes who aroused the greatest admiration.

In one saga, we read how the fair Oihauna refused to marry a king's son because he left his sword in its scabbard too much of the time. She exclaimed: "When shall I see the emflamed cloud spew forth the tempest? When shall I see you, oh handsome young man of my dreams, admidst the din of battle and the bloody glint of steel, truly display, before my eyes, the fire I have kindled in your heart?"

Ingeborg, daughter of a Norwegian king, was being avidly courted by Olaf, a young prince with a promising future but who had not yet proved his merits, and also by King Gotreck, whose much greater age was offset by his fame as a warrior. The young woman preferred the man who had already been a hero to his rival who might yet have become one, because in the words of the saga, "it is dangerous to buy an uncertain hope."

Though incapable of accomplishing great feats, the women of the North were proud to be able to inspire them and offered their favor as the prize for victory.

Harald with the Fair Hair asked for the hand of the beautiful Gyda, who pledged her love for him on condition that he should become king of the whole of Norway.

Harald accepted her terms, and vowed to let his hair grow until he had fulfilled them.

For twelve years he fought constantly against the petty kings, the *jarls,* and the chiefs who had the country divided up between them. He killed some of them, and subdued the others—all in order to win the hand of his beloved.

Besides the sagas, the ancient historians have left us a great number of strange and exciting tales of love and war, such as the following one, which is from a Danish chronicler. Two brothers, Hiall and Skate, had won fame as kings of the sea. Olaf, King of Vermeland, having refused to allow his daughter to marry one of them, they both challenged him to a duel. At his advanced age, Olaf could not hope to with-

stand these two formidable young men. Fearing for his life, he offered his daughter's hand to any hero who would spare him from the wrath of the two pirates by fighting them in his place. The duel was to take place on a small island, so that no-one could escape. The two brothers arrived with their companions. A stranger came forward and offered to fight on Olaf's side. He looked old and shabby, with the air of a common, undistinguished man. Yet he triumphed, killing both the pirates and their ten companions. His victory was acclaimed with wild enthusiasm in Olaf's camp—but with one exception: as soon as she saw the unimpressive dress and manner of her future husband, the princess fainted. Yet, when she opened her eyes, what a fantastic change had been wrought! What had looked like an old peasant was really a young prince, Alle, whose exploits were celebrated far and wide, and who had come specially from Norway to win the hand of a princess whose beauty was quite as famous as his bravery.

Having been raised with feelings of deep admiration for warriors who were renowned for their courage, Nordic women often sought to rival the heroism of their menfolk. The sagas contain more than one exploit performed by young women fighting in disguise as men.

The following episode is taken from the history of Sweden. A brave captain named Alle one day needed to assemble all his forces for a particularly difficult mission.

He then left, taking with him every man who was capable of bearing arms. A Danish officer, who was always watching for an opportunity to attack the coast of Sweden, learnt that, on account of Alle's absence, the town of Warend was undefended. This seemed to him to a good moment to ravage the country, so he quickly moved in with his seasoned warriors. His totally unexpected arrival caused a terrified stampede of women, children and the aged, who, unable to defend themselves, sought refuge in the mountains.

A girl named Blenda, calm and fearless in the midst of the general turmoil and panic, summoned a meeting of all the women from the surrounding areas by sending them the *budkafle,* a special stick which was used in ancient times as a signal for an important assembly, and which was passed from house to house. The alarm spread quickly and the women met in a hidden place.

Blenda then explained how she intended to save the country. Her proposals were adopted and the women disbanded, having promised to follow her instructions. She then left, accompanied by the bravest and most beautiful young women. She went to the Danish officer, and said to him: "You may take possession of Warend at your leisure. After all, our menfolk were wrong to go away and leave us all here alone and defenseless, without even saying whether they were coming back or not. Please avenge this cowardly affront, choose

44

us as your mates, you big, brave men! You will protect us. This evening, will hold a magnificent banquet in your honor.

That evening, the tables were loaded with food, and throughout the merry-making the tender, innocent-looking girls served the unsuspecting Danes the hardest liquor they could find. By nightfall, they were all helplessly drunk.

Then, on a signal from Blenda, all the local women, who had been lying in ambush armed to the teeth, quietly moved in, surrounded the captain and his soldiers, and ruthlessly massacred every one of them.

The women of Warend who had followed Blenda were rewarded for having saved the city by the granting of special privileges. They had acted like men, so they were given a man's share of their inheritance. Because of their courage in action, honors normally reserved for warriors were conferred on them on their wedding night; their wedding procession was accompanied by military music!

However, the women of nearby Nyndring, having promised to take part in the operation, took fright and ran away at the last minute. As a punishment for their cowardice, a humiliating tax called the *springskatten* (tax on flight) was levied at Nyndring for many years, right up to the 18th century.

If such was the bravery of the women of the North when their country was in danger, it will not come as a surprise to learn that more than one girl, impelled by a passion for adventure or by her love for some Viking hero, wanted to accompany him into battle, and be near him, whatever fate befell him, fighting at his side.

A singular example is Arlanger, the wife of Regner Lodbrog, who is said to have accompanied him on his last expedition, and even finished the last verse of his drapa, when the warrior's voice was choked by the serpents which were killing him.

In both history and legend, mention is often made of the wives of Vikings who were found dead at their husband's side on the battlefield.

The patriarchal customs of the peasantry, who were attached to their native soil, made no provision for women going to war. Among the Scandinavians the mother of the family, who had the key of the house and was in charge of the children, was surrounded with great respect. She had a seat of honor reserved for her at the table, and when the Vikings held a banquet the men usually waited until she had left the room before beginning to drink heavily, so as not to offend her ears with their bawdy conversation.

Mothers did not like the idea of their daughters going off with the Vikings, to lead a life of wandering which would make the domestic virtues difficult to practise.

The older, wiser men were worried that the girls might entice the already hot-headed Vikings to attempt some crazy endeavor,

such was their power over their menfolk.

Eventually, therefore, warriors wishing to enroll in Viking bands were required to take a vow of celibacy.

In the Saga of Frithiof, son of Helding, for example, a skalde exclaims: "The girls are safe on shore; they must not come aboard. Even if she were Freya, beware of the pretty young girl, for the dimple in her cheeks is a pit into which a man can fall, and her blond tresses, floating in the breeze, are a deadly snare."

The historian Wanderstrup writes of the participation of women in the Viking expeditions. "It seems surprising that so little attention has been paid to this important aspect, which had so much to do with the nature of their armies."

In support of this thesis he quotes from one source which described Viking vessels as containing *vast numbers of women and children,* though these words come at the end of a passage about the booty the Vikings were carrying off with them.

It is quite possible that, in the distant past, there may have been real Amazons, known as *skjoldmar,* or girls with a shield. But it does seem a bit far-fetched to claim that Vikings, just as they were about to put to sea on a long trip, would load the frail craft down with masses of women and children. One thing is true; the North-men looted everything as they went along, removing all that they could—men and women included. Some they would sell, and the rest

46

would be used as slaves. They hardly needed to take women with them on their voyages, as the towns they stormed and the countryside they laid waste were abundantly supplied with them. The famous Rollon, the man who defeated Count Beranger, having seized a young woman in this way, married her twice. Between the two marriages, he married the daughter of the king of France. His reasons for leaving one in favor of the other were political, not personal. The Vikings did not wish the people of their adopted countries to think of them permanently as conquerors; they wished to blend in, having allied themselves with the most powerful families. This is why they took care not to import Nordic women, of a strange race, alien to the language, customs and religion of the country in which they intended to remain masters.

4/ Regner Lodbrog, Viking and Skalde

After this general review of the way the Vikings lived, we shall now study some of the more famous of them a little more closely, and see how they are portrayed in history and in the sagas. *Saga* is from *zeggen,* which is cognate with the English *to say; legend,* on the other hand, derives from the Latin *legere, to read.* Whereas a saga is tradition passed down in words, a legend is a story which may have been read in a chronicle. The sagas are therefore older than legend; the oldest of them are particularly interesting.

Out of the mass of Vikings who kept appearing in a variety of countries from time to time, we shall choose two who will give us an idea of the others: Regner Lodbrog, who, in life and death, was a Viking and a skalde, and Olaf, who, having lived the life of a Viking, died a saint, and is still venerated as the patron saint of Norway.

It is perhaps true that Regner Lodbrog, like Roland de Roncevaux, owes his fame less to his historic accomplishments than to the wonderful adventures which the sagas embroidered around them. He had become famous by the sword, and also through his artistry as a poet. Unlike the French troubadour, the Nordic *skalde,* or bard, was not trying to delight the ladies at court with fables and love-songs: his art was addressed above all to the warriors themselves. He did not hesitate to follow the Vikings on their most perilous expeditions. The sound of his harp and his tales of war relieved the

49

Viking stone (Uppland, Sweden). Right: silver coin found in Gotland; it may be of Russian origin, and was perhaps brought back from an expedition.

tedium of many a lengthy sea-passage. He was himself present at the battle and took part in it, in order to bolster the warriors' courage, witness great deeds of prowess and entone the death song or *drapa* of the dying hero.

There is ample evidence of the high esteem in which the skalde was held by the Northmen; for example, Alfred the Great one day entered a Norman camp, disguised as a skalde, harp in hand. His enemies were so delighted with the songs of war that he sang, that it never occurred to them to ask what was doing there. He was thus able to collect valuable information which helped him win the battle next day.

Very often, the king himself took up the skalde's harp. Saxon the Grammarian mentions the strange case of a skalde who, by means of his harp, succeeded in winning the royal scepter. Saxon and Mersius tell how the crown of Denmark was open to competition, and offered as a prize to the best poet. Hiarm defeated his rivals and was made king.

Nordic scholars, such as Jessen and Steenstrup have studied Saxon's text, chapter 9 of which talks about Regner, and have tried to separate fact from legend.

However, modern scholarship has merely concluded that this hero was highly *enigmatic,* as Steenstrup puts it. This same author goes on to say "each time the critical historian tries to pin him down to a precise time and place, he slips away and re-appears at a distance. He seems to have all the features of heroes of fable and legend, and is a contemporary of several generations; he was a genuine Sosia during his life, and a ghost after his death."

Saxon the Grammarian deals especially with the military expeditions of Regner Lodbrog. Two Icelandic sagas are devoted mainly to his love-life.

It is a pity that, whereas history gives us few details, the sagas give too many, some of them being rather difficult to believe. However, we should not disregard legend: it is now thought that the sagas are more accurate than would have once seemed possible. Apart from this, they are interesting because of the insight they provide into the ideas, beliefs and lives of the Norman adventurers.

Historians place Regner in the 9th century. He was the son of Sigurd-Ring, whom he succeeded as king of Denmark. While he was busy making war against the Swedes, unrest broke out in his domains. The inhabitants of Scandinavia and Jutland had revolted, but the Seelanders had remained loyal to him. Regner arrived on the scene, defeated the insurgents and then, prompted by his wanderlust, he left his kingdom to seek new adventures elsewhere.

During his absence, some of his disaffected subjects elected Harald king in his place. Regner came back, drove him out, and then went off again. Yet again, Harald was elected king, and yet again Regner returned,

defeated him, and forced him to flee. The expeditions of the famous Regner are truly astonishing. The glint of his dreaded sword struck terror into his adversaries in England, Scotland, Russia, Germany, France and among the Greeks of the Hellespont. He killed several kings and distributed a number of kingdoms to his sons.

Scholars have tried, but in vain, to thread together the events of his life into some coherent sequence. After all, it is quite possible that the authors of these diverse and sometimes obscure narratives might have attributed the expeditions of several Vikings to a single man; especially as all the heroes involved, of whatever generation, were all more or less terrifying characters.

As for Lodbrog, let us repeat what the sagas have to say about this marvellous hero.

Froe, a Swedish tyrant, had killed the king of Norway and usurped his throne. Norwegian nobles, in rage and indignation, were determined to get their own back. Led by the fair Lothgertha, they joined forces with Regner, who was at war with Froe.

Examples of female heroism were not rare among the blonde young women of the north, who often followed the Vikings into combat.

At the moment of victory, Lothgertha won the heart of Regner, whom she had charmed with her courage as much as her beauty. However, before giving her hand to a man who, after all, had not yet proved his worth, she decided to put him to the test. She arranged to meet him one evening on a mountain where she lived. Her door was guarded by a vicious mastiff and an enormous bear.

Regner strangled the dog with his bare hands, and ran the bear through with his spear. He carried off his bride and shared with her the throne they had jointly conquered.

After Lothgertha had borne him a son and two daughters, he left her; conjugal loyalty was not his strong point.

A king named Heroth, while out hunting one day, had found a snake which he took home and tamed. Eventually, the snake grew to such a size that its daily diet consisted of a whole ox. He seemed to be in love with the beautiful Thora, the king's daughter. His jealousy was such that he used to follow her about everywhere, wrapping his coils tenderly about her body.

He was violently hostile to all would-be suitors of the young woman, and invariably

Viking vehicle (Denmark).

Wagon from Oseberg (Norway); primitive and heavy, but lavishly decorated.

sent a fatal dose of his venom coursing through their veins if they sought her attention.

Heroth made it widely known that he would give his daughter to any man capable of delivering her from this monster. Several handsome young warriors came forward, and all died in the struggle.

Regner, however, recognized no danger as being superior to his daring. He had some thick fur coats made, and, wearing them, he dived into the icy waters in mid-winter. The sodden fur quickly became a dense coat of ice. Regner then advanced on the serpent, sword in hand. The monster's venom slid harmlessly across the solid ice, and its teeth were unable to penetrate the iron of his shield. The fearless warrior sank his sword into the dragon's body and laid him out cold.

Thora ran to greet her savior. King Heroth, who had witnessed the entire scene from the top of a tower, kept his promise, but jokingly referred to Regner's strange outfit, and called him *Lodbrog* (*lod,* hairy; *brog,* coat)—the name by which he is known in the history books.

Thora gave Lodbrog six sons. When she died, he swore he would never marry again. This, of course, is the kind of oath that is most easily forgotten.

He then formed a most unusual army. He ordered his men to assemble the sons of the worst subjects in each house, together with those slaves whose loyalty seemed most suspect. With soldiers like these, he did not apparently feel much of a need for strict discipline. He established twelve judges—thus laying the foundations, in the opinion of some, for the English jury system. The slightest rebellion was harshly punished. He always shared out the considerable booty which he amassed among his comrades-in-arms.

One day, while his ships were sailing off the Norwegian coast, some of his officers, who had gone ashore, noticed a young shepherdess who had left her flock and gone to wash her ravishingly beautiful face in the sparkling waters of a fountain. Then, she loosened her splendid hair, which reached down to her feet. They reported back to the king that they had never seen such beauty.

At this point, the details given in the saga vary somewhat. According to one version, the king set certain conditions for the shepherdess to be received at his court, whereas in another, the girl accepts his invitation, but lays down her own conditions for doing so.

The Nordic people must love riddles: the Viking chief told the shepherdess to come to see him, but told her that she must be neither clothed nor naked, she must not have eaten nor be fasting, and she must be neither alone nor with someone.

The young beauty had no difficulty in resolving this strange problem, and told the king's messenger she was ready to follow him. She let down her blonde hair which covered her entire body and wrapped herself in a fishing net; she tasted a piece of leek and spat it out without swallowing it; and she went accompanied by a dog and not by a man.

Here is the other version: Regner had his men ask the young shepherdess her name, and invite her aboard. She replied that her name was Kraka; she turned down the invitation, and agreed to greet the king only after he had sworn to respect her, and not even to say a word which might jeopardize her virtue.

At the sight of Kraka, the Viking was full of admiration, and thanked Odin for sending him this divine consolation; he wanted to join his hand with the girl's as a sign of eternal union.

Kraka replied that the king would be in grave danger if he broke his promise, and asked to be taken back to her family. The king's passion knew no bounds; he described in brilliant colors the distinctions and glory which would be showered on her at court, where she would be the envy of all the other women. Then he had the most splendid, richly-adorned robes spread out before her, including a silver jacket which had once belonged to Queen Thora. But Kraka was unmoved by words and gifts alike. All she needed, she said, was an ordinary black cloth dress, in which she would look after her sheep on the beach, and try to please her ageing parents in their simple thatched hut.

The king insisted: all the northern countries had proclaimed him as the prince of heroes, and the bravest was entitled to the hand of the fairest. He begged Kraka to share his throne and his glory. His words began to have the desired effect. The shepherdess was now convinced of the prince's love for her; but could she be so sure of his constancy? Let him continue his expeditions for a while, and if, on his return, he was still faithful to his love, she would accept his proposal.

Wherever Lodbrog went the thought of his beloved Kraka was uppermost in his mind and drove him onwards to even greater glory. He came back more triumphant and more in love then ever. Moved by such fidelity, Kraka promised him her love, but insisted that her wedding should be celebrated in public, in the presence of the nobles, who would proclaim her as their queen.

Kraka was already the mother of four children, when Regner, who happened to be at the court of Uppsala, promised the king of Sweden that he would marry his daughter.

Was Kraka warned? In any case, when her not-so-faithful husband returned, she announced that she was going to reveal a secret that she had kept hidden for so long because she had been proud that he had married her solely for her charm. Her real name was Aslanga. She was the daughter

of Sigurd, whose fame is still alive in Nordic countries today. The destiny of her offspring had been foretold; and as evidence of the truth of what she was saying, she predicted that the son she was carrying within her would be born with the sign of a serpent around one eye. Events proved her right. Instead of asking the king of Sweden for his daughter's hand, Regner declared war on him, and Aslanga showed that she was worthy to be the daughter of a hero by sharing his dangers, and helping him in his quest for glory.

It would take too long to follow Lodbrog throughout his expeditions. He won renown from the Baltic to the Bosphorus, conquering whole kingdoms as he went along, yet settling in none of them.

After a long run of victories, Lodbrog's luck began to run out. Success had truly gone to his head; he undertook the conquest of Ireland with only two ships. King Aella defeated this minuscule force, and took Regner prisoner. The once-mighty king refused to give his name, and Aella condemned him to death in a pit full of vipers. At the approach of death, when he could feel the deadly bite of the hideous creatures, Lodbrog's courage did not fail him; he composed his own drapa.

"We fought with our swords. In the days when, as a young man, I was on my way east, to prepare a bloody prey for the ravenous wolves, the whole sea was like one huge gash, and the crows swam in the blood of the wounded."

"We fought with our swords. I tremble with joy at the thought that a banquet is being prepared for me in the palace of Odin. Soon, sitting in his magnificent dwelling, we shall drink mead from the skulls of our enemies. A warrior does not flinch in the presence of death. I shall not utter words of fear as I enter the halls of Valhalla.

"We fought with our swords. If only my sons knew the tortures that are now being

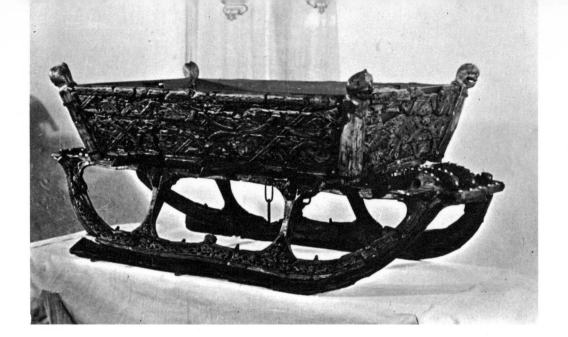

inflicted on me; if they knew that poisonous vipers were tearing apart my loins, how ardently they would leap to my rescue! The mother I have left them has given them a brave heart.

"We fought with our swords. But now my last moment is near. A serpent is already gnawing at my heart. Soon, the iron carried in my son's hands will be reddened with the blood of Aella and these brave young men will never seek rest thereafter.

"We fought with our swords in fifty-one battles in which the banners were flying in the breeze. Ever since my youth, I have learnt to keep my spear accustomed to the taste of blood, and I knew I would never find another king as valiant as myself; but now my time is finished. Odin is sending me his goddesses to lead me to his palace. In the front seat I sit and drink mead with the gods. The hours of my life have flowed away. I shall die laughing."

We have omitted some stanzas from this rather long death-song, but the harsh, grim passage we have reproduced, with its fierce images, gives a striking picture of the life-style of the Vikings. This drapa occurs in both Saxon the Grammarian and the earliest chronicles. Individual lines from the sagas have remained lodged in the popular consciousness. Torfoeus and Schoweng have heard phrases strongly reminiscent of this primitive poetry and the places made famous by the saga still have names which it gave them a thousand years ago.

Regner left several children. His sons helped him in his conquests and their own conquests were so numerous that an exact description of them is impossible. Their names occur frequently in accounts of the Norman invasions. They were terrifying warriors: one of them had himself burned alive on a bonfire made of the skulls of the decapitated enemy. The other ordered that,

58

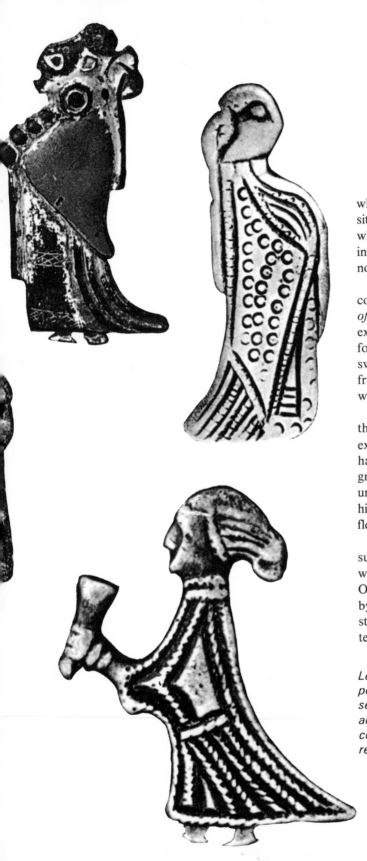

when he died, his burial-mound should be situated at the one point in the kingdom which was most exposed to attack so that, in his tomb, he could still be thrilled by the noise of war.

In the midst of his tortures, Regner was consoled by the thought that the *young of the wild boar,* as he called them, would exact a terrible price from his executioner for his death. His sons, Ingvar and Ubbo, swore that they would take the most frightful revenge for the atrocious agony which had been inflicted on their father.

They were as good as their word. In the words of Lingard, they enjoyed the exquisite pleasure of torturing the man who had killed their father. They showed even greater cruelty than Aella had, as they unhinged his ribs one by one, and tore out his lungs, pouring salt on the raw bleeding flesh as they did so.

Besides Odinism, there were all sorts of superstitions and idolatries in Scandinavia, which were more or less reconciled with it. Osten, king of Sweden, who was defeated by Regner, worshipped a cow whose strange mooing was capable of striking terror into his enemies.

Left: Norwegian sleigh from the Viking period. Facing: mounted warrior and several Valkyries (the goddesses who, according to the Vikings, used to welcome warriors slain in action, when they reached Valhalla.)

59

5/ Olaf, Viking and Saint

Saint Olaf, the patron saint of Norway, did much to establish Christianity throughout the kingdom.

In the north, the struggle between the religions of Christianity and Odinism was long and bitter; it lasted one hundred and fifty years and the final triumph of Christianity did not come until fifty years later.

Missionaries such as Saint Anchaire were sent from France by Louis the Debonair to preach the Gospel to the Vikings in their own country. And it was not by persuasive talk and example that the first apostles of the North succeeded amongst a people who worshipped Force; Christian kings imposed their will on their vanquished enemies and were obeyed. Should the power of these kings decline for any reason, their subjects promptly reverted to paganism, until the process of conquest was repeated.

Christianity first became established in Denmark. It was in the remoter parts of Scandinavia, however, that it took longest to destroy the gods of Odin—most particularly in the holy town of Uppsala, where their cult was strongest.

Few Vikings were as feared as Olaf Tryggveson, and few great saints have ever received the same kind of veneration and homage as he did.

A great number of churches were dedicated to him in the Scandinavian States, the British Isles, Holland, Russia and Constantinople. The Norwegian decoration created by Oscar I for a kingdom which

Motif on a runic stone, from the beginning of the Christian period. Right: funeral cross from the 11th century (Norway).

61

had no such special order is called the Cross of St. Olaf.

The Icelandic sagas tell of some marvellous adventures in which he was involved. The famous historian Steerstrup says that he was the son of Harald Granske, and a member of the royal family. When Harald died, his wife, Olaf's mother, was pregnant; when the future king and saint was born, she sent him into hiding in Sweden. The child was later seized by a Baltic pirate who sold him in Estonia. But Olaf was recognized by a member of his family, who brought him back.

His apprenticeship as a Viking started at the age of twelve, after which he learned the art of war by serving under King Valdemar of Denmark. Later he indulged his taste for piracy, fitted out a number of ships, manned them with Vikings and set off. He was to become the most famous Viking of all as a result of his exploits in the Baltic and on the open sea.

While still a young man, he took the Dutch town of Thuel, a prosperous trading center, sacked it and then burned it to the ground, in keeping with the Viking custom of destroying what they could not take with them. He has been praised for not burning down the church of St. Walburge, but he did profane it by smashing down the doors and carting off the sacred vessels and ornaments, which he could sell for a high price. With the money thus obtained, he quickly built up his fleet, and soon

returned with a powerful force of ninety ships. Having defeated the Dutch, who had taken up arms to put an end to his depredations, he marched on Utrecht, the seat of the bishopric. However, to deny the enemy shelter, it was decided to burn down the outlying houses. Olaf complained about this measure, claiming that his sole purpose in coming to Utrecht was to visit the bishop, whom he greatly respected, and to endow the church with wealth.

Naturally enough, Viking piety was far less well known than their devious ways of coming by loot. With a total lack of scruple, they were quite capable of asking to be baptised, the more easily to assassinate the bishop.

It is not clear from the writings of the monk of Drontheim, the panegyrist of Norway's patron saint Olaf, as to exactly where he was born.

Admittedly, the Saga of Olaf Tryggveson describes how he was baptized in a monastery, in the Scilly Isles, yet, according to another saga, he was baptized in Russia. English historians say that he was baptised in London by the bishop of Winchester, while his godfather was King Ethelred. On the other hand, Wace, the historical poet of Normandy, describes in detail the baptism of Olaf at Rouen.

As long as Olaf the Viking continued his life as a Viking adventurer, it seems that he could have been baptised several times, as the mood took him. Nevertheless, there

wide. He sailed north to Northumberland, and *amassed a great deal of booty*; then he wenth north to Scotland and *looted everything over a wide area.* Then he sailed on to the southern isles (Hebrides) and *killed many people there.* Then he went to the Isle of Man and *made war there. He caused havoc* over large parts of Ireland, after which he went to Bretland (Brittany), and *caused havoc* over much of that country, and also the country known as Kentland. Then he turned west to Valland (France) an *amassed a great deal of booty.* Sailing westwards he landed in England; after which he sailed on to the Scilly Isles, in the sea to the west of England." The skalde Halfrethur said that the young king Olaf *was merciless* and that the hero *killed* a great many people.

Hacquin the Bad, king of Norway, was so apprehensive about Olaf's ambitions that he arranged for a treacherous individual called Thor Klota to lure him into a trap, while at the same time promising to help him accede to the throne. Olaf discovered the plot, got rid of Thor and seized Hacquin's crown. Hacquin himself was slain by his own servants. According to some sources, Olaf met an abbot in the Scilly Isles who completed his conversion, which already been begun by a priest with whom he had been friendly.

Accustomed as he was to imposing his will by force, he said, "I want to convert my kingdom or die in the attempt."

was a time when his conversion was complete and sincere, after he had become king and sought to convert his entire kingdom.

Plunder was so much second nature to him, that when he landed in England he did not seem on the point mending his ways once and for all, and becoming a good Christian, as the following passage from the Olaf Tryggveson Saga shows: "However, Olaf Tryggveson turned towards England and *ravaged the country far and*

63

He convened a meeting of the people in order to invite them to embrace the religion of Christ. At first, he used the gentle language of persuasion, and, in a manner worthy of a Viking, he laid out the instruments of torture which were intended to punish those who might not see eye to eye with him. According to another source, king Olaf was constantly on the move throughout the various provinces, preaching, massacring and converting as he went. "The sorcerers' prophecies were all in vain, as he suppressed the revolt by burning the sorcerers." One day, when asked by the peasants to do what Hacquin had always done before him, he replied: "Very well, you want sacrifice, you're going to get sacrifice, but the victims are already chosen. They are not going to be low-level slaves, as in the past, the gods will find this offering *much* more to their liking".

Whereupon he hauled out of the audience the six most prominent and popular citizens. No-one was prepared to accept such a sacrifice; they all preferred baptism instead.

Once Norway had been converted, Olaf spread Christianity in France, Iceland and Greenland.

While the Vikings were ravaging France, burning down churches and butchering priests, French missionaries did not hesitate to seek out these cruel enemies in their remote land, to bring them the message of the Gospel.

64

6/ The Vikings in England

Since Sweden is close to Russia, the Vikings from that country figured prominently in the creation of the Russian nation by the famous Rurik.

Rurik was chief of the Vareg, a tribe of Baltic pirates, who were a sort of cousin to the Vikings. Indeed there were many Vikings among his men, and it was largely thanks to them that he succeeded in taking Novgorod.

There were three Viking—mainly Danish—invasions of England in the 8th Century. The main one took place in 787 when the Vikings, with three ships, put into one of the ports on the east coast of England. A local magistrate went down to ask the strangers their nationality and their names. In reply, the Vikings killed him, put the entire city to fire and the sword, and vanished, taking with them a rich booty. Soon they returned, this time with a larger force. They enrolled the indigenous people on their side, playing on their hostility towards the Saxons, and assembled an army large enough to worry Egbert, king of Wessex and Sussex.

Egbert set out at the head of a large army, to meet them, and scored an overwhelming victory. The defeated Vikings rushed in disarray back to their ships and fled.

They came back several times and, in 864, during the reign of Ethelred, took by surprise attack the city of Winchester, which they then plundered; one of their squadrons attacked the Isle of Thanet.

Motif on church door stile (Norwegian Viking art).　65

In order to be spared from Viking devastation, the inhabitants of Kent offered a sum of money, but in the words of Lingard: "no sooner had the North-men received the money than they mocked the credulity of the Savons and half the eastern province was plundered and devastated by these totally ruthless men."

According to Lingard it was about this time that Regner lived. As the reader will recall, at the moment of his death in the pit of vipers, he drew consolation from the thought that his sons would avenge his death. He was right.

Ungvar and Ubbo, his two sons, made themselves masters of part of England, and tried to conquer the whole country. They split up into two armies: one was based at York and took charge of the raising of crops on land which the natives had left fallow to deny the Vikings sustenance; and the other, much larger, army set off south and took Nottingham.

There was mass uprisings against these foreigners who had descended on the country like a diabolical plague; however, the thing that frightened the people most was not the military powers of the north-men, but their ferocious treatment of the most venerated priests and the violation of everything that was most sacred.

When they attacked, the sons of Lodbrog always saw to it that they had the element of surprise on their side; then they swept through in the still of night, committing atrocities wherever they went, particularly in the monasteries, while the blaze of burning farms and houses lit up the surrounding countryside as bright as day. The abbot of the monastery of Coyland had his head chopped off on the altar steps, and his monks were all butchered.

While storming the town of Medeshamsled, Ungvar was wounded. When Ubbo entered the town he was determined to avenge his brother's injury, so he personally slit the throats of a crowd of women and children, eighty-four monks and the abbot, who had taken refuge in the monastery.

After seiging Huntingdon, the Vikings moved to the Isle of Ely where the religious in the monastery were the victims of their atrocities. The leaders of the country seemed completely flabbergasted at the fury of these unknown invaders and did not dare resist, feeling that they might make matters worse. Seeing that he was outnumbered, King Edmond dismissed his men and sought refuge in one of his fortresses, but was captured and taken in chains before Ungvar. The royal captive refused absolutely to say anything contrary to religion and honor. He was put to death most horribly: he was tied to a tree and flogged, while his arms and legs were riddled with arrows. His sufferings were at long last ended when his captors beheaded him. This man of unshakable faith was later canonized.

Alfred, later known, and rightly so, as Alfred the Great, had succeeded his brother,

Left: Shields (9th century), which have been preserved in Normandy. Above: early map of England.

Ethelred, as king of the West Saxons. No sooner was his predecessor's funeral over, than the Vikings, whom he had defeated in battle once, re-appeared. They were never more formidable than when they were seeking revenge. Despite his military genuis, courage and vigor, Alfred realized that the

odds against him were too great, and that he could not rid the country of these fearsome invaders, so he came to terms with them and paid them an agreed sum for their departure.

The Vikings promised to leave and put an end to their plunder, but they took their

Exact reconstitution of a Viking vessel used for raids on English coast (Ramsgate, Kent).

own promises very lightly, and did not hesitate to seize their prey when the opportunity presented itself. Rich monasteries attracted their attention most especially. Despite their treaty with the king of Mercia, they did not spare the abbey which was dearest to the heart of the prince, Repton Abbey, which contained the tombs of royalty. The tombs were desecrated and the entire place was wrecked and burnt to the ground (874).

By 875, the Vikings had become masters of a large part of the territory of the Anglo-Saxons. In winter they went back home, and returned in the spring for another round of destruction, spreading terror and havoc far and wide. The nuns went so far as to disfigure themselves deliberately, so as to stand some chance of not being raped, though this did not guarantee them against other forms of cruelty.

In despair at his inability to dislodge them from Exeter, King Alfred tried to find some way of freeing his country from these invasions. In order to overcome the Vikings, he decided to play them at their own game: in 875 he fitted out some ships and manned them with mercenaries who then raided the Vikings on the open sea, thus greatly helping Alfred during his siege of Exeter, by destroying the Danish fleet, which had already been badly mangled by a storm as it made its way to Exeter to relieve the besieged Viking garrison. The formidable Viking Gottbrun, lost 120 ships and was

obliged to come to terms and withdraw to Mercia, where he began to cultivate land which he distributed among his veterans. However, while he seemed to be engaged in peaceful activities, he was really organizing a plan for a war to take over the last of the seven small Saxon kingdoms. During winter, which was usually the off-season for war, on January 6, 878, he assembled his men, on horseback, at a pre-designated spot whence they preceeded to attack the unsuspecting Saxons.

Alfred promptly despatched messengers, carrying a naked sword and an arrow, to all the villages of the kingdom, shouting: "In the name of the king and your homeland, which is in mortal danger, let all men worthy of the name come quickly!"

As no—one responded to his appeal, a desperate Alfred decided to rush at his enemies and die fighting; but, heeding wise advice he came to the conclusion that it would be better for him to withdraw from the political scene for a winter and wait for better times.

Through forests and swamps, this heroic and inspired king looked for a hut to hide in. Eventually he was taken in by a swineherd, who he helped in his humble dwelling. While her husband was absent, the lady of the house asked Alfred to watch the bread she had put in the oven to bake. Alfred, whose mind was constantly at work even when he appeared to be idle, forget to check the loaves and the bread got

Curious motifs on stone in Sodermanland (Sweden); the legend of Sigurd, in which he kills a dragon and consults the birds. Right: stele from Gotland (5'9" high).

Following pages: runic stone at Uppsala, and miniature depicting the Vikings attacking King Edmond of England (Pierpont Morgan Library, New York).

VALLSTENAR
VALLSTENA S
GOTLAND

burnt. The flood of wifely insults which this act of negligence prompted was a story the king often told with pleasure in later years. It was put into verse by his biographer, Asse.

Though frustrated by Alfred's disappearance, the Danes made the best use they could of his absence. Almost everywhere people chose to do their bidding, in the hope of calming their ferocity: Somerset was the only country which remained faithful to the king.

Several months elapsed before it occurred to anyone to go looking for the missing king. However, some of his friends did discover where he was and brought him news of goings-on in his kindgom, which he was always eager to hear. The invaders were feared because of the oppression they imposed on the people; yet the desire to throw off the Viking yoke was becoming daily more pronounced among his subjects.

In order to protect himself from unpleasant surprises, Alfred took up quarters on an island surrounded by swamps and dense forests, with a steadily growing band of supporters. From his island base, he made forays against the Vikings and also slipped into their midst, from time to time disguised as a skalde, and charmed them with his lively poetic imagination, while carefully noticing important details of their military set-up.

Alfred's supporters were now much more numerous; indeed, he found his island too small, and built a wooden bridge to the nearest firm land, defended by a fort.

Warriors loyal to Alfred's cause were now taking up arms on all sides. One of them, the ealdoman Odun, was eventually victorious. Among the booty collected after a prolonged and intense battle was the *reafan,* or 'Crow banner', woven by the daughters of Lodbrog, to which the Scandinavians attached immense importance. Crows were a prominent feature of the mythology of Odin, as their flight was thought to be a good or bad omen. If they flapped their wings it was a sign of victory, but a gliding crow which soared with motionless wings meant certain defeat.

Alfred now emerged as an avenging liberator of his country. At the head of a large army, he fought a long battle with Gothrum, the much-feared Viking chief, which eventually turned in his favor, and enabled him to cut off all possible retreat for the enemy, thus forcing them to capitulate. The two leaders, victor and vanquished, were both capable of magnanimity, after years of mutual admiration, with the result that peace was concluded between them and faithfully observed. Gothrum agreed to be baptized, and Alfred was his godfather. They recognized each other's status as king, and the extent of their respective kingdoms which were separated by the Thames. They both sought to live peacefully together and to establish harmony in the political and religious institutions of the two kingdoms.

Having won for Wessex the advantages of peace, Alfred then proceeded to show that he fully deserved the title "Great" by the wisdom of his administration quite as much as by his military successes. He acquired great authority over the petty kings, who eventually sought his protection and declared their allegiance to him. He died in 901.

His successors, however, failed to agree among themselves, and trouble broke out again. Then, during the fairly tranquil reign of King Edgard, a defensive fleet of 360 ships, in three squadrons, was sent along the coast each spring to protect the country against Vikings who usually sallied forth about that time, seeking adventure. The North-men were suitably impressed by these measures and turned their attention elsewhere.

The first Vikings relied heavily on the terror caused by their strange, barbarous appearance; but with the passage of time they became familiar figures and their would-be victims learnt how to foil their sudden attacks and devious methods. The spread of Christianity had led to a general softening of customs, and to advances in all the arts, including the art of war. Invasions were becoming more dangerous and therefore more rare, while the wandering life held fewer attractions than the sedentary life of a prince in peaceful control of a fertile land.

Vikings who landed in England now did so with much larger forces. Landings occurred in 980, 991 and the following years.

Two formidable invasions took place under a Dane, Sverd, and a Norwegian, Tryggvasson. In 1007 a fearsome new chief emerged; his name was Thurchill.

For three years, in three expeditions aimed at different parts of the country, he laid waste the richest areas, murdering and plundering mercilessly as he went.

The Archbishop of Canterbury, Elphège, was held in high esteem. Seeing that his city had fallen into the hands of the barbarians, the Archbishop, instead of fleeing for his life, was concerned only for the innocent people whose lives were in immediate danger; he rushed into the midst of the Viking band and begged them to stop the carnage. In order to stifle his voice, the Danes grabbed him by the throat, bound his hands, tore at his cheeks with their nails and beat him mercilessly with their fists. They inflicted every conceivable torture on him, while stopping short of killing him. Then they dragged him to his cathedral to witness a horrifying spectacle. The church was full of priests, monks, women and children, who had taken refuge there. Piles of firewood had been stacked against the walls; the Vikings then lit them and watched the blaze with shouts of delight. The flames rose to the roof, which soon fell in, sending blazing rafters and molten lead down onto the victims below. As they struggled to escape through the main

entrance, the Vikings butchered them one by one before the eyes of the Archbishop, and forced him to witness every detail of the lurid scene.

Elphege would have preferred to die rather than live through the horrors of that day in which his cathedral was burnt down and a thousand men died, not counting the women and children who were slaughtered in his presence.

The Vikings then locked him in a filthy dungeon, hoping to force him, by means of torture and abject terror, to pay a ransom for his life of 3,000 pounds. But the old man answered: "You're wasting your time; I am not the kind of man who would hand over the flesh of Christians for pagans to eat: and that is just what I would be doing if I were deliver to you what is intended to buy food for the poor."

One day, in the words of an early historian, when all the Normans had received kegs of wine from Denmark and drunk heavily from them, looking for some source of amusement after dinner, they sent for the old man. "We want gold, they shouted at him, all the gold you've got, and we'll make you famous throughout the whole world."

Foolishly, and probably because he was unaware they were drunk, the bishop started preaching to them, and offered them the gold of the divine word, threatening them with the most dire punishments should they

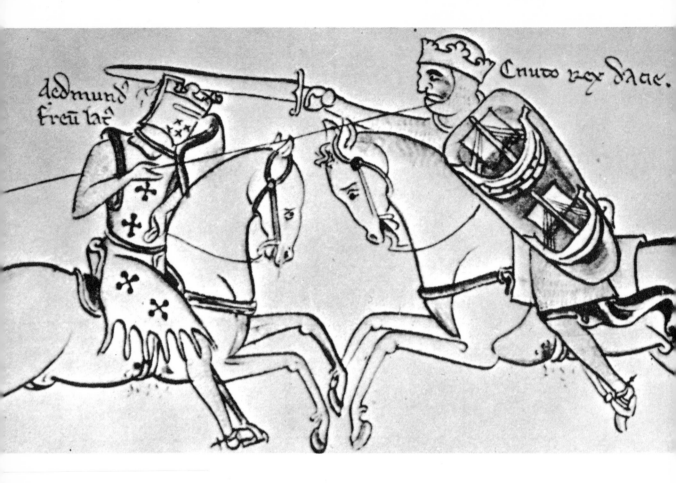

endanger his life. Hardly had he finished when the Vikings started roaring like wild beasts. One threw him a bone, another a stone and another an ox-head. The poor old man collapsed and they fell upon him beating him with their fists. He must have praised the Lord when, at long last, he succumbed to a merciful *coup de grâce* from a Dane whom he had himself baptized.

King Ethelred, as if wishing to reward Thurchill for laying waste the best part of

thirteen counties, gave him 48,000 pounds and welcomed him as a friend. The Viking swore allegiance to him, and many of them then settled in England.

Svend was angered by Thurchill's alliance with the very forces he was supposed to be fighting, and resumed the conquest of England himself. He laid siege to London, but the city was too well defended by the king and Thurchill. Even though he was less successful in besieging a major fortified

78

city than in his devastation of the country-side, the Danish king made such a far-reaching impact throughout the land that he was proclaimed King of the English, whereupon Ethelred prudently withdrew to the continent. The unexpected death of Svend, early in February 1014, seemed to him a good time to recover his throne, even though he had only just renounced it. The English hastily threw off the yoke of Svend's young son, Knud, who one day was to be known as Knud the Great, though he was still quite unknown.

Ethelred was received enthusiastically. Unfortunately, his vindictiveness and its consequences soon led to reprisals, where-upon the Danes could raise their heads again.

Then the great enterprise of the conquest of England as a whole was organized by Knud, with the help of all the best warriors the king of Denmark could assemble. The Vikings were certainly not short of funds as they had been amassing huge amounts of gold and other valuables from their raids throughout Europe.

We shall not relate here in detail the battles, sometimes of Homeric proportions which were fought during this campaign, right up to the gates of London. Eventually, the two sovereigns met and agreed to divide England with the Thames as the limit of their kingdoms. The Saxon was to govern the southern part, which was inhabited by the English, and Knud the north, where Danes were preponderant. The two kings embraced and swore eternal friendship. One month later, the Saxon *was visited by God,* as the chronicles put it, meaning that he died suddenly. It has been pointed out that this death was so well timed and so much in Knud's interest, that it seems highly likely he had a hand in it.

In any case he was proclaimed king of the entire kingdom.

At this point he renounced the fierce life style of the Vikings, and adopted the manner of a great king. He became sincerely Christian and brought about the complete triumph of Christianity in Denmark. In 1031, he made a pilgrimage to Rome, where he wrote a famous letter beginning with the following words: "Knud, king of all of Denmark, England, Norway and part of Sweden, to Egelnoth the metropolitan, to archbishop Afric, to all bishops and chiefs and to the entire English people, nobles and commoners, greetings!" Knud described his journey and said that he had come to Rome in order to beg God to forgive his sins. On Easter Sunday, there was a great assembly of nobles and important people who all received him with great honor and who gave him gifts. Emperor Conrad gave him gold and silver vases, rich embroidered cloaks and garments. "I wish it to be known to you all, he said, that I have devoted my life to the service of God, so as to govern my kingdom with equity and to observe justice in all things. If, in my hot-headed

youth, I have violated justice in the past, it is my intention, with the grace of God, to make amends for such actions."

He consequently recommended that justice be done evenly, to both rich and poor. He did not want injustices to be committed in order to fill his coffers, saying, "I do not need money raised by unjust means." He ordered that he be paid his due, plus St. Peter's penny.

He built religious houses and fine churches, particularly in those places where fierce fighting had taken place.

In order to win favor with the English, he married the widow of their former king Ethelred, Emma of Normandy, an intelligent princess who was fully conversant with the customs of the country of which she had been the legitimate queen.

Despite his conversion, Knud sometimes reverted to his fierce ways, but when he erred, repentance came soon after. He had granted great privileges to his guards and he had drawn up rules specifying the punishments for offenses against those privileges. The mere act of striking a guard was punishable by death. A guard who had been reprimanded three times was dismissed from the common table and had to eat alone; his former comrades, as a sign of contempt, could toss bones to him. Once, in a moment of anger, he broke his own rule and killed a guard. Stricken with remorse, he descended from the throne, assembled the entire corps of guards and asked to be judged by the rules of justice. He was asked to return to the throne and pronounce judgement on himself. He sentenced himself to a payment of nine times the price of blood.

A great deal could be said about the Viking invasions of Scotland or Ireland.

A particularly important event was Macbeth's victory over Sven Kanusson, king of Norway, whose army was literally hacked to pieces. As Macbeth has already been made famous by Shakespeare, a brief digression about his life is certainly permissible; moreover it will shed light on the thinking of a whole age.

Macbeth was related to Duncan I, King of Scotland, and was a man of unusual energy. One day, as he was travelling with his comrade-in-arms Banquo, three strange and mysterious women appeared in front of him. One greeted him as Thane of Glomis, the second as Thane of Cawdor, and the third as King of Scotland. Then, like apparitions from the world of the supernatural, the three creatures vanished.

Macbeth went to the king and was startled and thrilled to hear Duncan greet him as Thane of Cawdor. This remarkable fulfilment of the first part of the prophecy made him want to bring about the realization of all three parts. Between him and the throne were the sons of Duncan, so he could not accede to kingship through the normal line of succession. A crime was needed. In 1040, he received the king in his castle in Inverness and killed him.

When he then mounted his victim's throne, he won respect by combining firmness and generosity, but he could not rid himself of his constant, nagging remorse. He became wild, suspicious and cruel, and tried to wash his already bloodstained hands in fresh blood.

Superstitious ideas had played a great part in his accession to the throne; later those same ideas were to cause his death. He had been told that he would die only when the forest of Birnam Wood marched against him, and a man not born of woman struck him.

MacDuff, a powerful Scottish lord, had drawn upon himself the hatred of the tyrant, who had massacred his wife and children in order to punish him for his loyalty to the former king's children. He succeeded in making his escape, and persuaded Edward the Confessor to send an army against the man who had usurped the crown of Scotland.

Heavy fighting followed, as Macbeth put up a stubborn resistance; but his enemies exploited his credulous, superstitious mind. One day, the enemy force advanced with branches of trees on their helmets, and he was told: "It's Birnam wood advancing." He was terrified, as he thought of the prophecy which had been made. But when he learnt that MacDuff had not been born of a woman but of a corpse, as his mother was dead at the moment of his birth, he was paralyzed with terror.

Macbeth went mad, abandoned his soldiers and ran away, but he was captured and killed.

Soldiers and, right, "musicians", with trumpets ending in a wolf's mouth.

Vikings attacking a French town (11th century).

7/ The Vikings in France and Germany

During their struggle in the British Isles, the Vikings often had occasion to cross the English Channel, whether on account of some military reverse or in order to lull the suspicions of the natives before striking suddenly again. It frequently happened that they chose France when a campaign elsewhere had failed because of the rich booty to be won there and also because its internal discord made it an easier prey.

The first appearances of the Vikings caused widespread terror among the population. These totally unknown warriors from far-off mysterious lands, who came up past the mouths of the rivers on the tide, and landed at dead of night, rode off through the countryside plundering, looting and burning everything in their path, returned laden with their spoils, to their vessels which had been left hidden in some convenient inlet, and then vanished as suddenly as they had come.

Their fleet which were originally made up of frail-looking craft, were constantly growing bigger and stronger. Their long ships, with two white sails, a sharp prow, flat keel and menacing figurehead, were easily recognized when seen. The first invasions of these Barbarians who made it a point to appear as frightening as possible, left the simple countryfolk with the firm belief that these men had made a pact with the elements and with the Devil.

One day, Charlemagne, who was in Southern Gaul near Narbonne, was informed that some unidentified ships were approaching the port.

The Emperor rose from the table to see for himself. Standing on the balcony, he stared out to sea and quickly recognized the light craft with their special shape which could only belong to the northern pirates whom the French often described loosely as Normans.

When the barbarians were close to shore, they were asked where they had come from; as soon as they were told that the great Emperor was in the area, they turned and fled.

While Charlemagne was watching this scene, his face grew sad and tears welled up in his eyes. He then said to his astonished aides: "Do you know why I am upset? It's not because I fear any harm they might do to me. What disturbs me is that, during my lifetime, they dare sail so close; I can imagine the kind of trouble which they are preparing for my successors."

The great man was quite right. None of his sons were strong enough to wield power over an empire which stretched all the way from Elbe to the Ebro and the North Sea to the Calabrian Mountains. His descendants should have come to an understanding among themselves, in order to crush the invaders. Instead, they fought fraticidal wars to gain power for themselves, sometimes stooping to underhand methods in doing so.

Pepin II, king of Aquitaine, even made

a sacrifice to Odin to please the Normans. Carloman borrowed soldiers from them for use against his own father. Louis the Germanic, who was at war with his brother Hugues, the bastard son of Lothairef, had them fight in his army to help him win the crown of Lorraine.

Later, Louis the Debonair did much to protect the kingdom from this dreadful scourge. He ordered his men to block the mouths of the rivers which flowed into the ocean with ships. But the Normans were able to find a way of foiling such counter-measures, as their daring was certainly matched by their cunning. They made

frequent trips up the Seine and the Loire.

In 810, they attacked Tours and burnt the outskirts of the city, later moving into Paris where they were driven back.

In 819 a force of 30,000 Vikings arrived at the mouth of the Seine but, finding it too heavily defended they marched to the mouth of the Gironde. Séguin, Duke of Gascony, learned of the havoc they had caused on the islands of Oléron and Ré, and in Saintonge, and went to meet them at the head of a large force. Showing excessive bravery and insufficient prudence, however, he was killed in battle and the victorious Vikings sacked Saintes, Limoges, Angou-

The Emperor Charlemagne among his troops (early miniature).

lême, Bordeaux and the entire Basque country.

Hasting was one of the most famous of all the Vikings. In the old chronicles his name is spelt in ten different ways, and there is a great deal of dispute as to his origins. Schoening gives Norway as his birth-place; Suhin says he was born in West Gothia (Gotland, Jutland). Glaber, writing in the 11th century, claims that he was born in a peasant hut near Troyes, in Champagne. Glaber's opinion has been adopted by several French authors, in particular by Gabriel du Moulin, the historian of Normandy, and by Michelet, who states that Hasting was born in a village called Tranquille, three miles from Troyes, and that he belonged to the lowest level of the peasantry.

Whether Hastings was the son of a poor French or a Danish prince, he had all the quintessential qualities of the Vikings, even if he was not actually born one. He combined ability and courage, cruelty and love of adventure, treachery and deviousness, wisdom and loyalty, when loyalty was required of him by virtue of his position. Before making his appearance in France, he had made a name for himself in England.

It appears that he renounced Christianity for the religion of Odin. It has been established beyond a doubt that, in order to become Count of Chartres, he agreed to convert to Catholicism. This kind of calculating concession happened quite often among the pirate-heroes whose sole object of worship was in any case, Force. It would never have occurred to a Viking, while he was massacring monks and nuns in a church in the name of Odin, to ask them to reject Christianity for the religion of the gods of Valhalla. The Vikings often abandoned the faith of their fathers because it was in their interest to do so at a given moment; indeed they could embrace and reject it several times, as circumstances required.

The following anonymous anecdote was told by a monk from St. Gall. So many Normans had applied to be baptized that there was no time to make the fine robes that the newly converted usually wear, so a much simpler robe of coarse fabric had to be used. One of these was offered to a Viking, who rejected it indignantly saying: "Keep that sack for a goatherd; thanks to heaven, this is the 20th time I have been baptized and I've never been offered such rags before."

Another awe-inspiring Viking, Godefroy, built a fortress at Nimegue, founded a small Viking, settlement near Maastricht and, from his retreat, he went off on forays into the big cities. If he was defeated in battle, he would exact a terrible revenge by committing all kinds of cruelty and plunder elsewhere. *Inter alia,* he killed the natural son of Louis the German, devastated Charlemagne's palace at Aix-la-Chapelle and kept horses in the chapel which had been so lavishly and richly endowed with

CABALLI DENAVIBVS · E

Vikings landing in England, as depicted in the famous "Queen Matilda" tapestry, at Bayeux. Below, a view of the coast of Normandy.

pious treasures by the great Emperor.

In 845, a famous Viking named Roric went up the Elbe with 600 ships to attack the Emperor of Germany. He ran into such stubborn resistance that he decided to withdraw and try his luck elsewhere. He laid waste the coasts of Holland and Flanders and everything within his sight as far as the mouth of the Seine.

France was still torn by internal strife, so the Vikings thought the moment had come to attack Paris, the constant target of their ambitions. Yet this highly coveted prey was never to be theirs, as the city was very well defended and the bridge had been destroyed, thus making access difficult. The Vikings consoled themselves by devastating the surrounding areas; the abbeys of St. Geneviève and St. Germain-des-Prés provided a superb haul for them. Ragenaire, a much-feared Viking, famous for his plunder of churches, dropped dead while he was in the act of looting and desecrating a holy place. Everyone immediately thought a miracle had happened, and that he had been struck down by an invisible hand. The superstitious Vikings were convinced it was a miracle, so they handed back all their booty and prisoners.

The Vikings had several chiefs, and the rulers of the countries which they raided often found that, after concluding a deal with one of them, they had then to take into account the wishes of another.

Woland once went up the Seine with

Viking burial-ground.

ROLLON

Nous en resterons maîtres et seigneurs....

(25 Juillet 883)

200 vessels, when he was least expected. In order to stop him short of Paris, the king of France gave him 5,000 pounds of silver, sheep, cattle and supplies of wheat. According to some sources, the Vikings had already entered Paris and the king paid these amounts in order to get him out of the country.

Reduced to despair by their inability to defeat the Normans (this being the title now commonly given to the invaders from the north), they were only too ready to admit their impotence by paying a ransom to the very people they should have been sweeping ruthlessly from their country, exacting a high price for the damage they had caused.

The Vikings promised the central authorities that they would put an end to their destruction in return for an annual income of four thousand pounds (it is not clear whether they were of gold or silver). In addition, all prisoners of war were to be handed back (869).

In 870, despite the 4,000 pounds which they had been paid, the Normans were still on the banks of Loire. Hugues, an abbot, claiming to be president of all the abbeys of France, marched on the invaders with a band of man who had responded to his appeal, killed 60 of the enemy and took numerous prisoners (including a renegade monk, who was beheaded).

When the Normans left France in peace, they were busy wreaking havoc elsewhere.

The statue of Rollon at Rouen, principal city of Normandy; the words inscribed on the base are his famous remark (July 25 883) about the beautiful province: "We shall remain its masters and lords."

93

After leaving the banks of the Seine and the Loire, they went and burnt Trèves and Cologne.

A wave of terror swept through the land at their approach. Men and women were seized where they stood at work in the fields or towns. Rambert, Archbishop of Hamburg, worked hard to redeem the prisoners; he sold everything he owned, and eventually sold the sacred gold and silver vessels from the church, since, as he put it, it is better to save souls for God then have fine vessels for service in church *(Melius est animas Deo quam aurum servare.)*

With the accumulated wealth they now possessed, the Normans had no difficulty getting recruits. The loss of an entire army meant little, as a new, even stronger one could be raised quite easily.

The taking of Paris and the conquest of France remained, however, the prime goal of the invaders. The deaths, within a short time of each other, of King Louis of France, and of Louis the German seemed to offer them favorable circumstances in which to make one huge combined effort to succeed at last in this great undertaking, to which they aspired so much. However, despite all their successes elsewhere, this was one prey which was to elude them.

Though the names of many Vikings have slipped into oblivion over the years, there is one whose memory still lingers on, particularly in France: he is Rollon.

The spelling of his name varies; in Norway it is *Hrolf,* in Norman it is *Roll, Harotel, Rauoul* or *Rou,* in Latin *Rollus* and in French *Rollon.*

He was the son of Rogvald, a powerful Jarl whose wealth and ambition was of mounting concern to Harold Harfagher, King of Norway.

A historian from the abbey of Jumièges has described at some length a dream in which Rollon was invited to go to England and a vision which was interpreted by a Christian who told him of the glorious future which he could have in France.

According to Snorre Sturlesen, a Scandinavian historian, Rollon was a famous sea-king who was so tall that he never rode a horse since none were suitable for him—hence his nickname, Rollon the Walker. In France a *chevalier,* or knight, would never have fought on foot like a serf. Rollon's colossal stature prevented him from riding the small horses found in his country; as it happened his legs were quite as powerfully built as his arms.

In a great many documents Rollon is described as having led an extraordinary life. One of them in the *Roman du Rou,* a rimed chronicle, composed in 1160 by Robert Wace, which is one of the most curious monuments of the language and history of the Middle Ages.

After a spell in Europe, Rollon concluded a treaty of alliance with the king, and when they parted they embraced each other cordially.

Viking sword. The Vikings attack Paris (then known as Lutèce) in 845.

At first he behaved like a true Viking. He was opposed by some powerful lords: Reinier, Duke of Hainaut, and Rudbold, Duke of Frise, both of whom resisted his plunderous forays. The King of England, a faithful friend of Rollon, sent him 12 boatloads of grain, bacon and wine, and another 12 full of armed warriors.

One day, when attacked by a large force of Frisons, Rollon tricked the enemy into thinking he had few men by making half of them kneel down; when the signal was given, they all got up, their huge swords glinting in the sun. The victorious Vikings took many prisoners away with them on board their ships and levied a hefty ransom from the terrified populace.

Having forced his way into Escaut, Rollon laid waste the territory of Reinier of the Long Neck, Duke of Hainaut. Heavy fighting took place on several occasions and as the land was left idle, many people died of starvation.

Reinier was a brave, likeable fellow; one day, while lying in ambush he himself was taken by surprise, surrounded, and despite his resistance, he was led in chains before Rollon.

Meanwhile Reinier's men had captured many Normans. In the words of Guillaume de Jumièges, "Reinier's wife, weeping and lamenting her fate, summoned the chiefs and sent them to Rollon asking him to release her husband in exchange for his 12 comrades-in-arms. Having received her plea Rollon promptly sent her away saying: "I shall not release Rollon but I shall cut off his head unless you return my companions, and unless you hand over forthwith all the gold and silver in your duchy, under oath, and unless I am paid a tribute by this entire region."

The anguish-stricken woman did everything possible to save her husband at any price. She handed over the 12 prisoners and delivered to Rollon all the gold and silver she could get.

Rollon who behaved like a true knight when it pleased him, unfettered Reinier, asked him to be his friend, gave him half the gold paid for his ransom and returned him to his wife bearing an abundance of gifts.

The Normans left Escaut and put out to sea; shortly thereafter they sailed up the Seine.

Francon, Archbishop of Rouen and primates of the province then known as Neustria, realized that resistance was out of the question and that, instead of seeing his men butchered in a one-sided struggle, he would be better advised to come to terms with the enemy, thereby assuaging their ferocity.

He advanced to meet Rollon; and these two men, far apart in attitudes, found that a distinct mutual sympathy existed between them, and signed a peace treaty. This act was certainly a sign of things to come.

This cordial welcome led Rollon to value the wealth of Neustria and in particular,

The remains of the abbey of Jumièges, in Normandy, which was spared by Rollon. It was here that a chronicle of the Vikings' exploits was written.

to see the advantages of the geographical location of Rouen, which was well defended by an excellent citadel against attack from both land and sea.

Far from seeking to burn the city, he declared his intention to live there and make it his capital city.

Though he had an insatiable passion for booty, in common with other Vikings, he lacked their mad, sacrilegious hatred of priests and monks.

He spared the abbey of Jumièges which had been founded by Clovis I and deposited on the altar of St. Vaatz the chain and the relics of St. Hermentrude which he had brought from England or Frisia.

He withstood the Archbishop's efforts to convert him, but he did begin to win the sympathies of the Neustrians, by respecting their churches and their properties. This did not prevent him from continuing his forays, but at a distance. He also made an

attempt, like others before him, to take Paris, but to no avail.

The Normans arrived in Bayeux in 900, sacking the town by surprise as much as by force, since they were quite unexpected. They plundered the town and massacred the population. Their victims included Count Beranger, who left behind an unusually beautiful daughter, Poppa. Rollon fell in love with her, and despite some glaring infidelities, he loved her for the rest of his life, treated her like his wife and gave her two children; a son named Guillaume and a daughter, Gerloc or Adèle.

Feeling the need for some rest, Rollon briefly turned his attention away from military matters and began to show his genius as an adminstrator, by founding a Norman colony deep in French territory. He restored the fertility of the farmland which the Vikings had ravaged so many times, and consolidated the fortifications

Another view of the ruins of the abbey of Jumièges. Below: the meeting between Rollon and the king of France (stained glass, Viking period).

TRAITE ENTRE ROL... ...LES ...LE SIMPLE 912

of Rouen. The need for a strong government was becoming more and more obvious, as the authority of the king was in such an enfeebled state that he could not exercise real control or act to prevent disorder. The Neustrians rightly felt that their security would be better protected by the sword of a pagan than by the scepter of Charles the Simple.

Rollon eventually settled in Rouen and was elected king. His wisdom won him a wide measure of support among the people. Far from persecuting Archbishop Francon, he actively sought his favor; for from doing anything to harm the crops, he encouraged agriculture and made sure that those who worked on the land were held in esteem by the rest of the populace. He built forts to defend the country from outside attack.

It is true that whenever he left his part of France, the old Viking strain in him emerged. He had devised a form of far-reaching association among the Viking bands which were then scattered with a common leader, throughout France. His plan was to make himself the head of all the Vikings, and to begin by seizing all the wealth and able-bodied men of both towns and monasteries, so as to assemble a massive force with which to march on Paris.

France was in an increasingly deplorable state. The burghers were tired of repairing the towns, only to see them captured again, looted and wrecked; the farmland had been

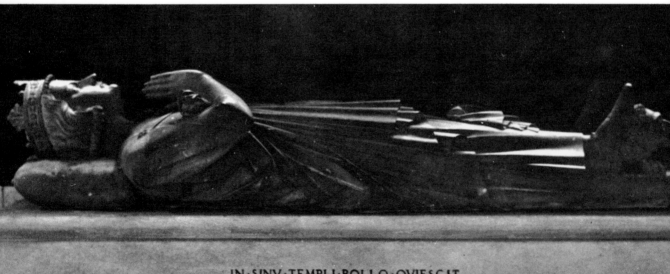

IN·SINV·TEMPLI·ROLLO·QVIESCIT
A·SE·VASTATAE·CONDITAE·NORMANNIAE·PATER·AC·PRIMVS·DVX
LABORE·QVI·FRACTVS·OCCVBVIT·OCTOGENARIO·MAIOR·AN·CM·XXXIII

abandoned by the terrified peasantry; indeed it was possible to walk for mile after mile without seeing the smoke rising from a single chimney, or hearing the bark of a single dog.

The only possible savior for the country was the man who had done so much to bring about its ruin. Rollon had to be persuaded to become a Christian and a French prince.

The king arrived at a decision only after consulting all the orders of the state, in the words of one chronicler. According to the *Roman de Rou,* he first consulted the nobles: "the bishops of France and all the high born, the barons and counts, old and young." In one ancient manuscript he assembled the states of the kingdom.

It was agreed that Archbishop Francon would offer Rollon Neustria, which would thereafter be known as the Duchy of Normandy, plus the hand of Gisèle, Charles' daughter. Rollon would be baptized and do homage to the king of France.

The Viking who had originally replied that he would obey no-one, allowed Francon to persuade him without too much difficulty. He readily accepted the hand of Gisèle and disowned Poppa. In any care the church regarded as null and void any marriage with a pagan, or one concluded without religious ceremony. This time he agreed to be baptized with good grace and promised to compensate the clergy for the harm he had done them in the past. However, he struck a hard bargain over the question of territory.

Normandy had been so severely devastated that Rolon found its resources were quite inadequate.

So Charles threw in Flanders. Rollon found Flanders too marshy and demanded Brittany, most of which was granted to him. His vassals were to include Beranger of Rennes and Alain of Dol. The Vikings had shown bad faith in the observance of treaties so often in the past that they, in turn, were highly sceptical as to whether their enemies would keep theirs.

When the deal was finally concluded, the king of France and the chief of the Normans, the former accompanied by his court and the latter by his knights and companions, held a solemn meeting in the village of St. Clair, at the boundary between Neustria and Ile-de-France.

Rollon swore allegiance to the king, using the traditional form of words: "Henceforth, *I am your loyal vassal and your man, and I swear to loyally preserve your life, your limbs and your royal honor.*" Charles then gave him his daughter, Neustria and most of Brittany, while Beranger and Alain swore allegiance to Rollon.

In the words of Guillaume de Jumièges: "Since Rollon had refused to kiss the king's foot at the moment when the king conferred on him the Duchy of Normandy, the bishops said to him: "When such a gift is given to a man, he must instantly kiss the king's foot." But Rollon was adamant. "I shall never bend my knee before any man, nor kiss his foot." Yielding to Francon's persuasion, he ordered one of his knights to kiss the king's foot, whereupon, seizing the king's foot, this knight raised it to his lips and, without bowing an inch kissed it, thus causing the king to lose his balance and fall backwards in an undignified heap, to the accompaniment of loud guffaws from the assembled populace."

Rollon's baptism was followed by the baptism of his entire army. The date was 912.

In this age of faith the clergy were very powerful in France, on account of their relatively high level of education and the veneration which was accorded them. For this most special of occasions, the baptism and marriage of Rollon, the full splendor of religious pomp and ceremony was deployed: after all, the famous warrior, so long the scourge of the Church, was now becoming its main bulwark, and moreover, he was entering the royal family after being for many years its worst enemy.

Archibishop Francon, who had never really doubted the genius and excellent qualities of the ferocious Viking, insisted on baptizing him himself.

After the sacrament had been administered, the Duke of Normandy stayed for 7 days (9 according to some versions) in his white convert's robes and, each day, made a special gift to a church in Rouen.

In those days it was customary for converts to wear the white garments they had received at the baptismal font for some time afterwards. It seems that when a Jew became converted to Christianity in Rome, his godfather was usually a cardinal, who, for two weeks, had the white-robed convert ride around with him in is his splendid coach with its red plumes.

Rollon's wedding followed close upon his baptism. This union between the Duke of Normandy and the daughter of the king of France was no ordinary occasion, and all the principal vassals of the crown were summoned to attend.

Rollon's most famous lieutenants now stopped their adventurous mode of life and became, like their leader, Christians and French. Charles the Simple, who had frequently been on the receiving end of their military prowess, now received their pledges of loyalty and homage, and gave counties to Gelon, Botton and Hebert. According to Guillaume de Jumièges, Rollon distributed his territory among his followers by drawing straight lines across it.

Those who wished to continue their adventurous life, or simply to go home to their country, were given lavish presents.

Rollon's most immediate concern was to repair the harm he had done to the clergy and the country which were now under his rule.

Having destroyed churches, he now built many splendid new ones and restored

those he had damaged. The chronicles are full of praise for his sincere devotion and his ardor in the service of God.

The brutal, fearless warrior was still present in his soul, but he was also truly gifted. He saw that it was his prime duty to restore the security which the Viking invasions had destroyed everywhere, so that his people would multiply and prosper. From the very beginning he realized that the clergy could help him immensely.

The relics of St. Ouen, which were deeply venerated in Neustria, had been moved away to central France, where they would be safe from the Vikings. The king would have preferred to keep them, but Rollon demanded them back in a tone which allowed of no refusal. The Duke of Normandy, barefooted, followed the procession which brought the body of St. Ouen to Rouen.

Gisèle, a princess of the blood, who had been raised at the court where the traditions of Charlemagne were still alive, was not happy being married to a Viking, whose ways were distinctly *not* those of the French court.

She died childless, and Rollon then married Poppa for the second time. He regarded her son Guillaume, who was already a young man, as his future heir.

The face of Normandy now changed quickly. Farmers who received fertile land without burdensome conditions cultivated it diligently. Farmers who were not themselves war like were anxious to settle in Rollon's domains because they felt that he was powerful enough to protect their crops against the threat of renewed invasion.

Fugitives from all countries could confidently seek asylum from the Duke of Normandy, who was disposed to be lenient towards those with a record of plunder, murder and arson, provided, of course, that they were prepared to change their ways.

Rollon created a court of justice known as the *Echiquier;* he enacted laws and enforced compliance with them.

What source did he draw on for these laws?

Did he model them on the laws of Denmark or were they a formal version of the ancient common law of the province?

The Danish historian Steenstrup believes it would have been out of the question for Rollon to impose French laws on his subjects.

On the other hand it seems equally impossible that having become a French duke and a prince of the royal family, the Norwegian Rollon should have drawn on Danish law, which was relatively undeveloped at the time. Moreover, his French subjects already had a body of common law to which they were deeply attached and which closely resembled that of other provinces of the kingdom. At the time of Charlemagne and Louis the Debonair, legal science was much more advanced in France than in Denmark, and it seems certain that Archbishop Francon was a better legislator

than the Viking Rollon.

The laws of Rollon, which were not in writing, have been lost. The oldest written collection of the laws of Normandy, the *Vieux Coutumier de Normandie,* had no definite date. In it we learn that Rollon recorded the ancient usages and customs and consulted the wisest men, who knew what had always been done.

Nevertheless, in the enforcement of those laws, the newly converted Viking sometimes showed a streak of brutality strongly reminiscent of his old barbarous ways.

Guillaume de Jumièges has the following to say:

"Rollon published a law applicable within Normandy, making it an offense for anyone to help a thief: if caught, both thief and helper were to be hung. Shortly afterwards, in the Longuepète area, a certain farmer, wishing to lie down and rest, stopped work and went back indoors, leaving his scythe, plow, and other tools in the fields. His wife who was quite distressed and over-wrought removed all these things without telling him, in order to test the Duke's new law. When the peasant went back out into the fields and saw that his tools were missing, he went to report the matter to the Duke and ask his help in getting them back. The Duke was moved to pity by the man's story and paid him compensation of five sous, besides which he ordered a search for the lost tools throughout the neighboring towns and countryside. Eventually the peasant's

wife was arrested and beaten until she admitted her guilt. Then the Duke turned to the peasant and said: "Did you know all the time that she had stolen them?" When the peasant replied: "Yes", the Duke added: "Your words have damned you, wicked servant." And he had them both hung from the gibbet.

Rollon was both feared and loved. Yet his sword remained in its scabbard, except to subdue an armed revolt by disaffected Bretons.

One of the chronicles claims that, on his death-bed, the Duke of Normandy, being a former Viking, sought to ensure that he would enjoy the favors of the gods of both his old and his new countries, so he sacrificed a hundred Christians to the Northern gods and gave 100 lbs of gold to the churches of Normandy. Such an occurrence, however, would have contradicted all that we know about the religious feeling of Rollon after his conversion. According to Richard de Poitou, before he became converted to Christianity, Rollon sacrificed 100 Christians to the idols he was about to forsake.

As is well known, the Viking's French province of Normandy was the base from which they, as Normans, set out to conquer England, thus fulfilling an ancient dream of their forefathers.

106   *A Viking vessel as seen by Arab eyes, in an early miniature (New York Metropolitan Museum).*

8/ The Vikings in Spain, Africa and Italy.

The Viking's quest for new and promising sources of loot was certain, sooner or later, to lead them to the Iberian peninsular. There they found an abundance of riches, but they also met with much stiffer resistance.

The Arab historians who recorded the invasion of the northern pirates did not write their versions until the tenth century; their work was based not on the reports of eye-witnesses, but on an assortment of often confused traditions which in many cases were mutually exclusive.

For this reason, scholars seeking to unravel the tangled mass of dates and events found in the various chronicles have been faced with insurmountable difficulties.

Rather than embarking on learned and obscure dissertations, we shall choose, among the different versions, those which are most commonly recognised as authentic.

A Norman band is thought to landed twice on the west coast of Africa, at the point where Arcilla was later built. In 844 or 845 the Arab governor of Lisbon warned the Emir Abderraman that a fleet of fifty-four ships and an equal number of sloops had brought a force of Vikings (*madjou*, or pagans, in Arabic) into the town.

After a stay of three or seven days, depending on the chronicle one consults, the Normans left Lisbon, and went to Cadiz and Seville.

Abd-el-Rahman was one of the Emirs of Cordoba who were most renowned for their power, prowess and magnificence. Within a perimeter of eight leagues Cordoba contained sixty palaces, four thousand shops, nine hundred public baths, six hundred mosques and seventy libraries. His main palace was without equal anywhere: it was supported by four thousand columns of marble, and was adorned with precious wood, marble inlays and ornate gold and blue motifs, with splashing fountains and a pool containing a superb gift from the Emperor of Constantinople: a golden swan crowned with a magnificent pearl.

The progress made in agriculture and industry, the famous leather made in Cordoba, the six thousand silk-weaving establishments in Seville, the sheets of Murcia, and the manufacture of paper had combined to make Andalusia a very rich place indeed.

As soon as the Emir was warned of the Vikings' approach, he acted to stop them; but he can hardly have been aware of their ferocity or their numbers.

As usual the Vikings laid waste everything in sight as they advanced inland. On September 29 845, the Muslims marched to meet them, and were beaten. They now realised that they were up against no ordinary bandits. The madjous pressed on, plundering as they went, stopping only half a league from Seville. The alarm in the city was complete: the entire population took up arms to defend it. Despite their bravery, and because of the Vikings' tactical advantage of having taken them by surprise, the Arabs were routed.

When this unexpected news reached Abderaman, whose title was the Victorious, he promptly recognised the gravity of the situation and organised his own system of defense. He chose as commander in chief of the cavalry a man whose courage and prestige were so great that all the Muslims immediately rushed to join him "as closely as the eyelid is joined to the eye."

Heavy fighting ensued between two armies which were fairly well matched in numbers and prowess. At last the Arabs were victorious ; they killed five hundred Vikings and burned many of their ships, having first removed everything of value from them.

The head of the Viking chief, together with two hundred other severed heads, was sent to the inhabitants of Tangiers as a gift from the Emir. The defeat of these madjous was hailed as a glorious accomplishment, especially as it had saved the region from further unspeakable horrors.

The sheiks of Seville complained that the barbarians spared nothing. They shot flaming arrows into the exquisite mosque, leaving deep scars on the walls and floors; it was claimed that the only thing that saved the temple from the fiery destruction

Viking helmets.

108

*Artists impression of
a Viking landing.*

which the Vikings usually visited upon such places of worship was an angel which was sent by Mohammed!

The Vikings were in no hurry to reappear in Spain. Indeed, they stayed away for several years, in order to be the more completely forgotten.

The date of the second Viking invasion of Spain is placed somewhere between 858 and 861. This time the pirates from the north raided the islands of Majorca, Formentera and Menorca, left them virtually empty and moved on to Greece, which they left after three months and sailed back north again.

On June 23, 966, El-Hakem, Caliph of Cordoba, was informed of the sighting of a fleet of 80 Viking vessels off the Atlantic coast. In those days, each one contained about 80 men. The madjous began by plundering and devastating the plains of Lisbon. The Muslims engaged them in battle several times, with heavy losses on both sides, but little in the way of decisive victory.

On their return the Vikings entered Navarre, capturing Pamplona, and with it, the king, who was released on payment of a ransom. The Viking invasion of Galicia, where the northerners were greatly feared, has been more thoroughly recorded in history.

Sisenando, bishop of Compostela, was afraid that the accumulated treasure deposited in the sanctuary over the years by devout pilgrims might fall into their barbarous hands. In 961, he asked King Sancho for permission to surround the great Apostle's temple with a system of thick ramparts, ditches and towers. Once the royal approval had been obtained, he immediately started building, putting to work not only slaves and vassals, but also persons normally exempt from heavy physical toil, such as priests. When the Vikings, having laid waste the coast of Galicia, landed near Santiago, the entire population rose to confront them. In 1012, the city of Tuy was wrecked by the Vikings, under the orders of the famous Olaf, son of Harald.

According to the saga, Olaf, conqueror of the pagans, (this time meaning the Muslims) was waiting in the Bay of Cadiz for a suitable moment to cross the straits, when he had a dream which altered all his projects. He dreamt that he had seen an awe-inspiring man of majestic bearing appearing to him in a vision, saying to him: "Go back to your country, where you will reign in Norway for ever."

And it is fact true that, as patron saint of Norway, his influence over mens' souls in that country was to be profound and long-lasting.

Ulf, who was described in one saga as a terrifying Viking, ravaged Galicia once again and left for home, laden with rich spoils.

The Vikings who had settled in France, in what was now being called Normandy, had kept some of the traits of their forefathers, despite their more refined way of life, and their commitment to certain interests; they still dreamt of adventure in remote lands. A chronicle written in Barcelona by Ademar tells how Roger, a knight from Normandy, arrived in Catalonia in 1018, with a force of hardened warriors.

He entered the service of Ermecinda who was governing Barcelona as regent until her son came of age. He won great esteem by virtue of his ability and courage. He fought the Saracens, just as the Vikings had fought the Christians, with the same audacity and pretty well the same methods.

Besides spreading a more conventional kind of terror, by sheer ferocity in combat, he exploited the dread which the northerners had always inspired. Some strange stories were told about these wild men, who had once been cannibals and were thought to be still, at least by some people. Ademar has the following story to tell in this respect: "The Normand brought in by Roger to fight the pagans in Spain killed large numbers of Saracens, and captured many towns and castles from them. Quite early in the campaign, Roger hit on a trick which would have a tremendous impact on his opponents: in the presence of Moorish prisoners, he had his cooks put quarters of corpses, rather than pork, into a steaming cauldron on the fire; the dish

112

was brought to him at table, and he went through the motions of enjoying a lovely meal. The prisoners who witnessed this spectacle were naturally horrified. They were then released and went off to report the monstrous things they had seen."

"Such was the terror caused in the Muslim camp by this news that they promptly offered to accept Ermecinda's terms for peace, and agreed to pay her tribute." Cunning was not the only Viking trait Roger had, however; he was also fearless. Ermecinda gave him her daughter's hand in marriage since he had proved his worth by performing brilliantly in battle against several Muslim princes.

As they became more civilized, the Vikings lost none of their daring and love of adventure; instead of fighting Christians, however, they had become defenders of Christianity, and covered themselves with great glory and distinction in the Middle East during the Crusades, and in the wars against the Saracens in Spain.

On their return from the Holy Land, they described to their compatriots the splendors

of the Byzantine court, and the wonders of a country which was completely different from the cold north which was their home.

The passion for the Crusades then spread throughout the north. In 1103, Magnus the Barefoot, king of Norway, was killed in battle in Ireland, leaving his states to his three sons. One of them, Sigurd, is known as *Jorsalafani,* or 'he who has been to Jerusalem'. In 1107, he left for the Holy Land with sixty vessels and a small army. Tghough the journey was a long one, Sigurd does not seem to have shown any desire to shorten it, as he did not take the most direct route.

The Vikings often stopped along the way, spending one winter in England, and the next in Galicia, the *Jakobsland* of the sagas. The shrine of St, James at Compostela was still one of the most famous in the whole of Christendom. After landing in Galicia, Sigurd asked the governor of Galicia for foodstuffs, for which he offered to pay. The governor could easily fail in his obligations to an ordinary pilgrim and get away, it, but not with Sigurd, who, under his Crusader's breastplate, still had the heart of a Viking. The governor cheated him on the deal: Sigurd in reply killed the governor, and carted off to his ships all the foodstuffs and money the castle contained.

Shortly afterwards, he had the good fortune to meet some Saracen pirates. After a battle, he seized eight of their

ships, and chased them ashore to the fortress of Cintra, which belonged to the Moors. He took the town and put to the sword every single Muslim in it, because they refused to become Christians. Here again, we have the traditional Viking method of conversion—baptism or death.

The Vikings felt that they could reconcile their love of looting and plundering with the principles of their new faith by concentrating their ferocity on the enemies of Christianity. They were to re-appear in Italy. Hasting, for example, having longed to conquer Paris and London, decided to take Rome instead.

Dudon de St. Quentin, at the abbey of St. Jumièges, and other chroniclers, tell us that Hasting was in command of the Vikings who entered the Mediterranean in 861 and ravaged the coast of Italy. The fierce Viking was not much of a geographer, and, when he reached Luna, (now Luneggiano), he thought he had reached his ultimate destination. This town, which had flourished under the Etruscans, still had some of its former grandeur, even in the early Middle Ages; indeed, when the Vikings saw it, they were sure it was Rome.

Seeing a strange fleet just off shore, the astonished citizenry barricaded the gates to the town, fortified the ramparts, and prepared for a tenacious resistance, in the words of the monk of Jumièges.

Hasting realized that a frontal assault would be costly, so he decided to take the city by devious means. A delegation of Vikings, speaking the local language, and peaceable in appearance, asked to see the count and the bishop. They said: "We are foreigners who have just come from France and have been thrown onto your shores by the tempest. We want your hospitality and we will pay you handsomely for it." Since this opening statement met with a cool reception, the Viking added: "Our chief, broken by old age, is suffering and close to death after a long illness. He would like to receive baptism before he dies, because, while in France, he learnt to know and love the Christian faith."

On hearing this the bishop listened with new interest, and allowed their chief to be baptised in the cathedral. The ceremony was held with every pomp, in the presence of a huge throng, anxious to see the foreign prince. Hasting, wearing a purple robe trimmed with gold, was leaning on a stick, as if he could barely stand up, and was propped up by this officers.

The next day, cries of anguish and grief were heard coming from the moored Viking craft; word had spread that the old chief was dead. The Vikings went to see the bishop, saying: "Our chief has just died. His last wish was to be buried in the cathedral where he was so happy to be baptised. He has bequeathed a great amount of wealth to your cathedral in order to have masses and prayers said for the repose of his soul."

It would have been hard to refuse such a touching request from a dying man. The bishop himself decided to be the celebrant. The foreigners were allowed to get food, but they were not allowed to come into the town armed. Several of them were granted permission to carry or accompany the body to the church and attend the funeral. Several more slipped surreptitiously into the cathedral or the streets. All of them were wearing breast-plates under their tunics, and had concealed weapons about their persons.

The bishop was in the midst of the funeral ceremony, the crowd were on their knees. All of a sudden, the gold cloth covering the coffin rose; Hasting stood up, sword in hand, attacked the bishop and the count and killed them both, and then signalled for the Normans to spring into action fully armed. Then Hasting and his men gave vent to their ravenous fury on the defenseless crowd. The church was the scene of unspeakable crimes; both young and old were butchered, the town was devastated and the ramparts were razed to the ground.

One wonders whether this could have been a true adventure; the truth is sometimes stranger than fiction...

After this triumph at Luna, the Vikings under Hasting were now determined to correct their original mistake, and really find their way to Rome.

They inquired about the way to the city, and particularly about the distance; they met a pilgrim who told them: "You see the

The miniature shown below depicts a Viking king from the 12th century: the age of conquest has now come to an end, and Scandinavia is entirely Christian; the king is in the company of a bishop.

shoes I am wearing and the ones I have on my back? Both were new when I left Rome, but the journey is so long that they are now both worn out."

True to form, the Vikings did not press on with this difficult undertaking, and preferred easy loot to glory, so the idea of the conquest of Rome was abandoned. Many years passed before the Vikings were seen again in this part of Europe. However, they were later to defeat no less a power than the Pope, who confronted them at the head of his armies. Two Viking chiefs, the Guiscard brothers, became Italian nobles; one was made Duke of Pouilles and Calabria, and the other Grand Count of Sicily.

Artist's impression of Viking craft sailing in the waters off Greenland.

9/ The Vikings discover the New World.

The northern pirates, while out at sea looking for booty, often found themselves on wholly unknown shores, of which they took possession. For example, they discovered thirty-five islands which they called the Faroes (from the word for ewe) because their flocks fared very well there.

In 861, a Norwegian navigator, Noddod, on his way back from the Faroes, was driven by strong winds towards unknown shores. He found a territory covered in snow and called it Snowland. A Swede, Gardar Svarfarson, recognized it as an island and called it Gardarsholm.

That same year, or shortly thereafter, the Norwegian pirate Floki Rafa was well out to sea, in dense fog, and had lost his bearings. His released three crows, the birds the Vikings dedicated to the gods, and watched to see which way they would go. The first returned to the Faroes, where the ship had just come from. The second came back and perched on the mast, and the third took a direction which Floki Rafa followed and which led him to the land which he named Iceland.

The ice shone brightly on all the mountain-tops, standing out all the more brightly against the lava flows. Floki soon grew to dislike this grim, icy place, with its dense, damp forests and decided against colonizing it. In the words of one historian: "curiously, his companions reported it very differently; they found the climate remarkably mild and the soil very fertile.

The milk flowed from every plant, and butter from every blade of grass. Domestic animals could spend the winter there without the need for shelter: the rivers were full of salmon, and the nearby seas full of whales; this was the land of wealth and liberty."

Shortly, afterwards, Ingolph, a Norwegian jarl, decided to go to Iceland with his brother-in-law Hiorleif in order to escape the vengeance of an enemy; as he left he took with him the door-frames from his house, tossed them into the sea, and vowed to settle wherever the waves took them. This seems to have been a Scandinavian custom: Stockholm was built on the spot where such a piece of wood was found. It was felt that fate, or the gods, would thus designate the site of a future city.

Ingolph landed on the island called Ingolphshodi, and settled at Faxofjord, where the frames of his doors had been found by his slaves. The colonization of Iceland dates from this moment. Hiorleif settled at a point on the southern coast, which still bears the name Hiorleifshodi. His death was tragic; the native slaves lured him deep into the forest during a bear-hunt and killed him. Ingolph avenged his brother-in-law's death and began to exploit whatever wealth the island had to offer. However, the discovery of Iceland led to that of Greenland; intrepid mariners who often sailed in the waters off Iceland set off looking for unknown land, guided by the

flight of birds which suggested the existence of land to the west. No danger could deter their insatiable passion for adventure in remote places. They discovered Greenland. More than a hundred years passed before this discovery could be put to use. About 986, Eyrik the Red, who had been banished from Iceland for murder, sailed off with Herjulf Braddsson, towards Greenland, which they colonized.

Herjulf's son Biarne, who had left this country seeking adventure on the high seas, one day came back to Iceland hoping to find his father there. To his astonishment, he was told that his father had left in the spring of 968, to settle in Greenland, after first selling all he possessed. Without unloading, Biarne set off immediately to look for his father in regions which were quite new to him. He spent a long time at sea, being forced off course by the strong north winds, and finding it impossible to navigate by the stars because of the thick fog. When, eventually, the sky did clear, so that he could navigate more easily, he saw land which did not correspond at all to the descriptions of Iceland which he had been given. First, he came upon wooded country dotted with small hills. Then, a plain covered with trees, and, lastly, he saw the island, surrounded by tall mountains and glaciers, which he had been looking for. This was where he stopped and was reunited with his father.

When he got back to Norway, Biarne's descriptions of the uninhabited lands he had passed while lost in the midst of the ocean, and his regret at not having visited them, aroused the imagination of his fellow countrymen, who were always eager to embark on new adventures.

One of those who found Biarne's accounts of his travels most exciting was Leif the Good; son of Eyrik the Red who had discovered Greenland in 989. Wishing to emulate his father's discoveries of far off lands, he bought Biarne's boat, recruited thirty-five fearless mariners, loaded plenty of cattle and supplies for the colonisation of the new lands and set sail about the year 1000. The first land he visited was covered with jagged rocks and boulders with little vegetation, so he called it *Helluland* (rocky country); experts think it must have been Newfoundland.

Leif did not stay long there and soon he moored his craft near flat wooded country which he called *Markland* (land of forests) and which, judging by contemporary accounts, must have been Nova Scotia.

This means that Leif discovered the New World. In fact the Vikings were to visit North America several times before Columbus ever sailed from Spain.

Once he had reached the New World Leif continued his quest for adventure and landed on a high green island, with a very gentle climate: Nantucket Island. Contemporary descriptions of his voyage are perfectly accurate and correspond closely to the present appearance of the areas visited. For example, off one particular coast, Leifs vessel was stranded at low tide; and there is a sandbank just at that very point on modern charts. He is also reported to have found a river the shores of which he called *Furdustrand* (wonderful shore); in fact, modern travellers have noticed a remarkable thing: through the mirage effect, the dunes which extend for a long way along the sea front do seem to reach up to the sky.

With his companions, Leif went back on board the vessel which the rising tide had now floated off the sandbank, and dropped anchor in a river which flowed out of a lake. This is presumed to be Rocasset River, which does in fact flow from a lake.

The Viking navigators found the mild temperatures in these parts a pleasant contrast to the harsh climate of Iceland and Greenland, and decided to spend the winter there. There was plenty of fish and game; birds laid delicious eggs on the ground. Today some of the islands, where large numbers of ducks and eiders have their nests, are called Egg Islands.

Their cattle thrived in the lush pastures which were all around. The absence of

adbuiat. descendens au ad hiemale solsticiu. similit
taõe fac au ff lib. hi ignorantes pagani. era illã uo
cant scam. 7 beatã q̃ tale miraclm pster mortalib.
Itaq; rex danox e multis aliis testat ÷ h ibi otingi
sic in suedia 7 i noruegia q̃ i ceris q̃ ibi ñ infulis.,
Pretea unã adhuc regione (insulam) recitauit a multis i
eo reptã oceano q̃ dr winland. eo qd ibi uites spo
te nascant uinu optimu ferentes. sla 7 fruges ibi
ñ seminatas habundare ñ fabulosa opinione s; eta
oxim relatione danox. Ite nob retulit be

---

snow during the first winter, the mildness of the climate and the fertility of the land were such that the voyagers stayed on for some time in this beautiful part of the world, of which they were the first inhabitants. One of them, Tyrke, discovered slopes covered with wild vines; he let the grapes ripen and made a splendid wine, hence the title Vinland (*Vinland in Gotha*, the good country of the wine), which the Vikings gave to it.

Modern travellers have since confirmed that grapes do grow wild on these hills.

The precise data which the Viking explorers recorded about the length of the day, and the number of hours the sun remained on the horizon have given us enough astronomical information to make it certain that Vinland must be situated in the states of Massachusetts and Rhode Island.

In spring, the navigators returned to Greenland and told of the marvels they had seen. Leif's brother Thorowald was eager to learn all the details of the first expedition and later embarked upon a second himself, landing in Vinland in 1002 with thirty intrepid companions. From there he conducted his explorations for three years. A number of early manuscripts suggest that he went as far as Maryland.

Thorowald had spent two years in Vinland without ever seeing any sign of human life. He was taken very much by surprise when his camp was attacked by a group of short dark-skinned men with wide, ugly faces and filthy-looking hair. These were the Eskimos, who in winter used to emigrate to the south; they travelled swiftly across the seas in canoes made from animal hides. The Vikings easily repelled their attackers, but Thorowald was killed in the struggle.

In 1006 a Norwegian, Torfinn Karlsefne, was a guest of Leif in Greenland. He fell in love with his host's sister and married her. He had been deeply impressed by Leif's account, of his time in Vinland. Being of a similar adventurous strain, Torfinn decided to try some new ventures of his own in this unknown land. After the preparation necessary for a long voyage, he set sail, taking with him sixty men and five women, among them Freydis, the natural daughter of Eyrik the Red.

The savages who attacked Thorowald, and whom the Vikings called *Skroelings,* appeared again in Vinland during the Winter. Torfinn realized that it would be in his own interests, in this unpopulated country, to come to terms with the periodic invaders and become their friends, rather than having to repel their attacks. He set up trading relations with them, receiving, in exchange for items of little value, some very valuable furs. For example, he traded a piece of fabric a few feet long and one finger wide, for a baby seal fur. The Skroelings were still in the Stone Age, and were not civilized. Their only weapons were made of flint: they were amazed to see an iron axe cut so easily through wood and

yet blunt its edge altogether on stone. They had no cattle or other livestock and no agriculture.

One day while the Vikings and the Skroelings were peacefully trading, a bull which had been brought from Iceland suddenly emerged threateningly from the forest, bellowing with rage. The Skroelings leapt into their canoes and vanished.

One day, three years later, a whole fleet of fast boats appeared off shore. Armed men jumped ashore and rushed inland howling a fierce battle-cry as they went.

Torfinn used the bellowing of the bull as a counter-measure. In fact the Skroelings had come determined to fight this animal which in their eyes was a monster, and they sent a shower of spears in its direction.

The ensuing battle was fierce and one-sided, as the Vikings were heavily outnumbered, to the point where even Torfinn decided to retreat. At this sign of weakness Freydis cried out "How can men with a brave heart flee from such wretches who are as easily killed as sheep? If only I had a weapon I would show you how to fight!"

Being in a late stage of pregnancy Freydis could not keep up with the fleeing warriors. She seized the sword of a dead man, stopped, suddenly turned round, and confronted the attackers, with bare breast, a wild look in her eye and brandishing her sword aloft. This sight was too much for

the Skroelings who turned, in terror, and ran back to their canoes.

In 988 a powerful Norwegian lord named Marsson was driven ashore on the coast of Hvitramannland (Land of the White Man), which is now thought to correspond to the territory of North and South Carolina, Georgia and Florida. Are Marsson won a name for himself in the unceasing wars which the indigenous peoples fought amongst themselves, and was elected king of a tribe.

The Vikings and their descendants sailed over most of the world's seas. The Norwegians founded colonies in countries which were least susceptible to any form of civilization; by 1347 they had travelled along the coast of the American continent, and visited unknown lands long before the more famous voyages of discovery were made; they had passed the Davis Strait, and entered the Lancaster and Barrow Straits.

Recent discoveries have proved that the Scandinavians went as far as South America, and formed settlements there. Excavations in Bahia, Brazil, have produced a flagstone covered with ancient Icelandic characters, traces of dwellings similar to those of Northern Europe and a statue of Thor, with all his attributes; hammer, gauntlets and magic belt.

In several parts of the New World, particularly on the east coast of Baffeen Bay, stones bearing runic inscriptions have been found.

Reconstitution of a drakkar. *Below: statue of Leif Erikson, discoverer of the American continent, at Saint Paul, Minnesota.*

Below and right: two Viking ships preserved at Oslo.

10/ Viking boats

Scandinavian boats varied greatly in mode of construction and dimensions, each particular type of boat being designated by its own name.

First comes the *Holker,* (Old Norse Holker) from the word *Holk.* This boat was little more than a hollowed-out tree trunk, as can be seen from the Old Norse name.

These craft, which were like canoes, were used only in the fjords and not for distant expeditions. A more advanced form came into being much later on, for use as a sloop, so that when a large Viking man of war arrived off some foreign coast, this smaller craft could be instantly lowered and provided access to shallow inlets and tidal flats.

This more advanced version of the Holker must clearly have served as a lifeboat for the crew of larger warships. Furthermore they could be taken ashore easily and even provided shelter for their occupants on dry land.

As the Norwegian historians tell us, the range of boats used by the Viking comprised all dimensions, right up to the big warship known as *Langskibe* or *Skeider.* The first title lays stress on the great length of the vessel, whereas, the second means "fast war sail-boat".

There were also merchant craft which, unlike the warships, were squat, as the sagas tell us. They were built more for the carrying of cargo than for attack or defense; and were known as *Knarr* or *Knöre.*

Remains of a Viking vessel at Oslo.

Then came the *Snekkar* (serpents) or warships which had about twenty seats for roasmen. They were also know as *Drakkar,* or dragon. The etymology of this word is *Drage* (the modern Danish-Norwegian *dragon*) and *Kar,* meaning vessel. Nowadays, however, the word *Kar* is more commonly used to mean a vase, and less often in the sense of ship.

This name derives from the fact that these ships frequently bore the head of a dragon on their bow. One source describes them thus: "A sort of vessel with the shape of a dragon, with a very long structure, with ornate dragon motifs." While one cannot be entirely sure as to its mode of construction, we may nevertheless infer that it was a very long vessel, and that its outer surfaces, which were probably covered with painted scales had wing-patterns on its sides; on the forward part of its hull, at the water-line it had feet with terrible pointed claws, at the end of its prow a hideous dragon's head, and, on its erect sternpost, a dragon's tail which would be either straight or twisted.

Another kind of ship was the *Trane,* from the Scandinavian root for 'crane'. The vessels, in particular, those of the kings and powerful chiefs, were sometimes lavishly decorated after a successful raid. According to Ericus Olaus, King Kanut had a dragon of prodigious size (60 oars), adorned with gold and silver figures.

Reference is made to another which

Two Viking boats which long lay buried in the earth: a) in Denmark and b) in Norway. The latter was discovered in 1903 near Oslo.

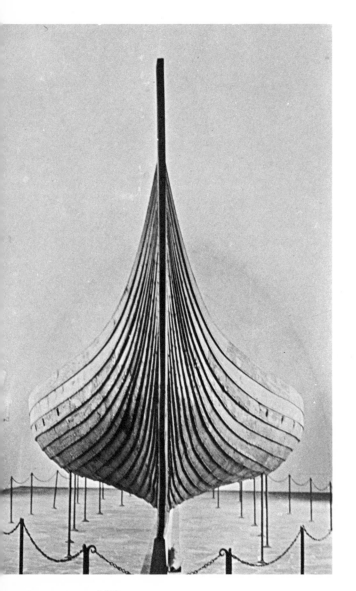

"looked like gold, glistening in the splendid rays of the sun which it reflected over the ocean waves."

According to William of Malmesburg, Godwin gave the king Harde Kanut a vessel adorned with gilded metal. Beauvois mentions a saga which describes ships with a gilded prow and sculpted sternpost.

Another Norman chief had his ship adorned with gilded sails, on gold-plated masts, with purple rigging.

It is quite certain that the chiefs used to adorn their ships and took great pride in their appearance, since the brilliance of their decoration, particularly on the prow, served as a distinctive means of identification.

It should be noted that such luxurious adornment had to be earned and truly deserved; the chiefs were not entitled to embellish their vessels until they had won a victory over the enemy. Their dress also was exceedingly simple until they had proved their merits in combat. They were all supposed to be basically equal, and it was only natural that their ships should be so too.

On August 18, 1863, the remains of a well-preserved ship dating back to the time of the Scandinavian expeditions was discovered at Nydam, near Österstrupp, in southern Jutland. It was lying in a northwest-southeast direction (fig. 1).

This ship had an overall length between the highest points of the stem and stern

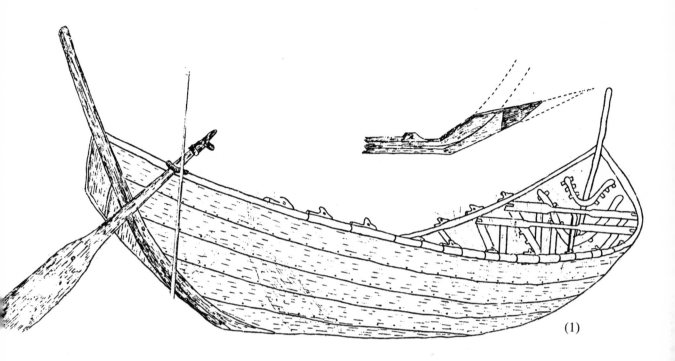

(1)

of 75 feet, it is quite broad amidships, about 11 feet. It is a remarkably elegant vessel, with great beauty and suppleness of line.

It is built of ten oak planks, five on each side. These planks are joined together by iron nails, eleven inches apart, with a rounded head and a rivet-end.

The vessel is built clinker-style, with a method of linking the planks to the frames which is unlike that in use today.

The planks have an overall length of 40'3", and are of a single piece. The fore and aft ends are held in place by means of wooden pegs.

The prow and sternpost both have large holes through which ropes could be passed to haul craft out of the water. We should remember that, in the late Iron Age, boats were always brought ashore in winter, and were rarely left moored in creeks, especially for the feast of Iol, which fell on the winter solstice.

There are no decks, not even a fo'c's'le or quarter-deck. Both stem and stern are pointed, with so sign of a mast. It is propelled solely by oars, of which there are fourteen pairs.

The rowlocks are of a special sort which were still in use in Norway in the last century. Although these so-called rowlocks served the same purpose, they were coarsely fashioned and not constructed in quite the same way as the modern variety.

(2)

(3)

It seems extraordinary to us now that these rowlocks had to be held in place with straps, which means that they had to be re-adjusted quite often. However, such a system, despite its apparent defects, and the one big merit of making it possible to switch the oars, so as to go forwards or backwards.

On the side of this vessel there is a rudder measuring 7'4" with an opening in the middle, through which a rope must have passed.

This is a very old type of rudder, which remained in use until the about the middle when it was shifted to the central aft position it is in today. In the Bayeux Tapestry it still occupies this earlier position. It also appears on a bas-relief of the Leaning Tower of Pisa, as well as on various early documents and seals (fig. 2, 3).

The oars found in this vessel are very similar to those of today, with a length of thirteen feet. Amongst other items of equipment found on board was a big iron another, and two scoops.

In 1855 a remarkable discovery was made in a burial mound at Ultune, in Sweden. This burial mound contained the unmis-takable remains of a vessel in which a warrior had been buried with his weapons and his two horses. The iron nails in the hull were still in position.

Its size was that of a small vessel. Next to the burnt body was a sword: its blade was of iron, and its magnificent gilt-bronze handle was adorned with exquisitely elegant filigree patterns. Fragments of the wooden scabbard and its gold trim were also recovered.

Other items found at the same site were: an iron helmet with a bronze point trimmed with zinc, a splendid bronze-plated iron boss from a shield, the handle of the shield, 19 arrow-heads, the bits from two bridles, a pair of scissors, all of iron, and a set of 36 drafts and three dice made of bone.

In the forward section was an iron grill and a cauldron made of riveted iron plate with a movable handle, together with some pork and goose bones, which were probably the remains of the funeral dinner.

It was at this time in Norway, about five miles from Frederikstad, that the splendid ship now preserved at Christiania was discovered.

It is made almost entirely of oak, built clinker-style with iron nails; the exceptions are certain pins and small parts which are of fir.

The keel, which is in a perfect state of preservation, is 44' long. The total overall length of the vessel been estimated to be about 75 feet.

There were certainly ten or eleven planks on either side. Some fragments of the tenth plank still remain. The planks are about one inch thick and vary in width from 6-12". One of them, the 8th from the bottom, is much thicker than the upper ones, being two inches thick and five inches wider.

The Bayeux tapestry gives us a very clear idea of the way the Vikings controlled the sail and rudder.

It seems likely that this plank, which is stronger, thicker and wider than the rest, was meant to provide greater solidity and, perhaps later a more reliable defense.

The nails securing the planks of the hull are riveted on the inside, being round on the outside. They are spaced 7-10" apart.

The joints in the planks are made water tight with tarred hair.

All of the long planks which make up the hull are bevelled and joined by means of three rivet-nails. Since the gunwale is missing, the rowlocks are missing too.

There are thirteen frames; the end ones are missing and some of the remaining ones are in poor condition. They consist of three kinds of wood and are joined partly by iron nails or wooden pins; the upper and lower layers are of oak, while the central layer, which is broader than the others and juts out slightly on either side, is of fir.

At the bottom of the boat, there is a heavy rectangular piece of oak which rises above the five middle ribs. This piece of wood has a square opening just aft of the middle rib, for the mast. Facing it is the thick block of wood which supports it.

When this vessel was discovered, more than two inches of mast, of fir, were still in position.

It is obvious that the construction of this boat was expertly and meticulously performed. Each plank of the hull is adorned with a net-pattern carved in the wood, inside and out. The same pattern and certain moldings occur on the upper side of the rib.

At several places in this vessel, a kind of light blue paint seems to have been poured over the wood. After much research and conjecture as to the nature of this paint, it was concluded that the color is merely an iron compound in combination with an iron oxide which the surrounding earth had deposited on the wood during the hundreds of years the ship lay buried.

About seven miles from the seaside resort of Sandfjord, in southern Norway, on a property owned by Gokstad, was a burial mound known locally as the King's Hill *(Kongshangen)*. In 1880, this was the site of the discovery of a boat which probably dates back to somewhere between the end of the 8th and the middle of the 9th centuries.

The ship had been lying in the earth with the stem facing the seas. It must be remembered that, in those days, the sea must have been much closer to the burial mound than it is now. It may even have lapped against the foot of the mound.

The boat had been placed in this position so as to enable the chief to put to sea easily when the Great Father called him to the paradise of Scandanavians, Valhalla.

The boat (fig. 4) is made of oak. The planking is kept in position by means of round-headed nails with an inner riveted tip (fig. 5).

There are twenty ribs, (fig. 6) the upper face of which is joined to the hull by means of iron nails and wooden pins. Caulking is done with cows' hair in three strands.

The keel (fig. 7) is a single piece of oak, with an overall length of 57 feet with a width amidships of one foot. At either end, the keel is joined to two pieces of curved wood which form the prow and sternpost, both of which were built in exactly the

Another Viking sail, and an anchor.

same way. Of the two, however, the sternpost is distinctly taller.

A great deal of good taste went into the design of this vessel, as can be seen from the three filigree patterns which run the whole length of the keel and which occur also on the planking of the hull, both inside and outside; finely carved moldings are also to be found on the rib.

137

There are no seats for the oarsmen, so one may assume they rowed standing up; this is a fair assumption when one considers the length of the oars which were found in the vessel. These oars (fig. 8), which were sometimes extremely long, passed through holes about 1 1/2 feet below the gunwale, (fig. 9). The oars were inserted in the holes from the inside, as can be seen from the slots, situated next to the holes, which allowed the blade of the oar to pass through.

When the oars were not being used, and so as not to ship water, the holes were closed by means of wooden flaps (fig. 10), on which there are some exquisite mouldings which must have taken a great deal of patience and skill.

The gunwale, which is about 4-5 inches thick, is partly missing.

Sail was used as well as oars, as can be seen from the pedestal of the mast, a 6-ft. section of which is still in place.

A slot about 5 1/2 feet long in the mast-block was probably meant to enable the mast to be lowered. Moreover, there are two pieces of wood which could be used as a winch when the mast was being raised or lowered. In the middle of the mast, about 6 feet up, there was a wooden cross-piece 3' 9" long and 7 1/2 inches thick, which could be used to erect a tent covering the occupants of the boat and its contents; indeed, it was customary to protect the boat in this way when they were moored in coves or bays for any length of time, since the Vikings often used them as temporary dwellings. This simple mast-structure was common in the Nordic countries for many centuries (fig. 11).

Scandinavian vessels had only one sail, as can be seen from the most authoritative sources.

The sails of the ships which carried the Vikings on their expeditions were made more and more luxurious as the pirate in question amassed wealth from the plunder of abbeys and towns; rather than a simple sheet of canvas or specially thinned animal hides, they often had sails of gilded fabric, like those of Ingell, or with brilliantly painted colors.

According to Guillaume of Malsnesburg, Harald, king of Norway, gave King Athelstan a vessel with a purple sail.

The chiefs had emblems, rather like the medieval coat of arms, which they had painted on the sails of their craft; they often included animals and, in particular, the crow—the bird which, the Vikings believed, had the power to predict the future. It was also an ill omen. In most cases, the crow was painted on the standards which were situated on the starboard side.

Another custom was the placing of a weathercock on the top of the mast, both as a means of telling which way the wind was blowing and an as an ornament.

Shields were sometimes used as signals.

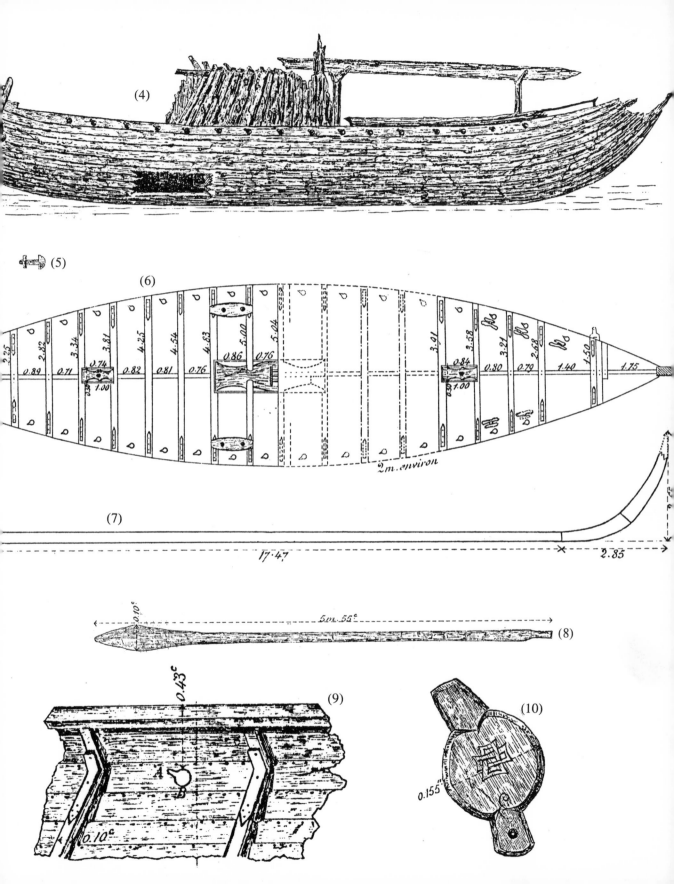

(4)

(5)

(6)

2.25
2.82
0.89   0.71   0.82   0.81   0.76
3.34
3.81
0.74
1.00
4.25
4.54
4.83
0.86   0.76
5.00
5.04

2m. environ

3.91
3.58
0.84
0.30
3.21
2.68
0.79
1.40
1.50
1.75

(7)

17.47   2.85

(8)

0.10ᶜ   5m.55ᶜ

(9)

0.43ᶜ

0.10ᶜ

(10)

0.155"

(11)

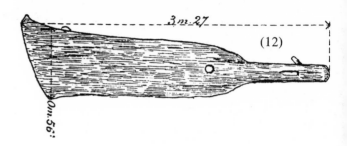

(12)

For example, a king named Hithim used to hoist a shield on his mast in order to let everyone know that a friend was approaching.

The rudder (fig. 12) seems very similar to other specimens previously discovered. It is attached to the last rib of the aft section of the boat, about 18 inches from the gunwale.

The upper end of the rudder handle has a longitudinal opening which used to accomodate a helm (fig. 13) which was found in the boat. It is a beautifully made piece, the thick end of which is in the form of a fish's mouth. A rope was passed through a roughly made iron ring situated behind the rudder, on the lower part of the blade. This rope was used to hold in securely in position, to maneuver it and to raise it slightly out of the water when the need arose, so as to reduce its effect on the steering of the vessel.

All the discoveries which have been made show that, in the time of the Vikings, it was customary to bury a chief in the boat which had carried him on his expeditions and which was meant to serve him for ever, after death, and carry him to the doors of Valhalla, to the Scandinavian paradise which the dead warrior would enjoy the life to come and its pleasures which consisted of vast, daily combats, at the end of which all those involved, both victors and vanquished, would sit down at a merry banquet in the palace of the god

Odin, where the Valkyries waited on table.

Not only did the Vikings bury the chief in his boat, they also put in with him the animals he had owned: his horse or horses, which he could also use, as he wished, to go to Valhalla. His treasures accompanied him to the grave in the form of the number of objects which were in his possession. It has even been suggested that, besides his favorite animals, some of his slaves might also have been sacrificed in his honor.

However, one can not form a clear idea of the religious ceremonies which they held because all that has been found at such sites is calcified bones, which proves that cremation was common.

Sometimes, the body of the chief was placed on his boat, which was then set alight as a funeral pyre and launched into the sea, where the Viking warrior and his craft sank into the element which was never to leave them, before or after death.

Women were often given the same burial as warriors; this is not surprising when we remember that many of them went into battle at their husband's sides and attached quite as much importance as they did to the martial virtues.

Early shipbuilding materials, carpenters (12th century, Norway) and work on board, from the Bayeux tapestry.

*Prow of Viking craft (British Museum)
and exhibition hall in Oslo.*